CONSTRUCTION SCRUM

How to Deliver Projects Easier, Better, and Faster

ISBN: 979-8-497-72166-9

Library of Congress Control Number (LCCN) : 2021917079

Edited by Bettina Deda

Illustrations by: Lilian Bello
Book Design: Michael Neon

Publisher: Better and Faster LLC

City of Publication: Sheridan, Wyoming

DEDICATION

This book is dedicated to my favorite product owner, partner, and best friend, Ali. Her ever-present backlog has guided our family to achieve well beyond our sprint goals. Equally, I am forever changed by the best developer I know, my son Noah. He helped me recognize the value of being present, planning for tomorrow, and enjoying limitless learning and play.

Dr. Jeff Sutherland and the entire Scrum Inc. team know how sincerely grateful I am for their contributions and partnerships over the years. Without Jeff and Ken and their commitment to inspecting and adapting Scrum, I wouldn't be thriving in the construction industry since 2014.

I sincerely appreciate the whole construction industry. Mentors, coaches, and friends have supported and trusted me while experimenting with Lean Construction and Scrum projects worldwide. Equally important are the skeptics that have provided priceless feedback and constructive doubt to help me refine and improve my approach, methods, and engagement with people building our world on design and construction projects everywhere.

My vision for this book is to bust the myths and assumptions around Scrum and simplify your life as a construction project manager, superintendent, field engineer, executive, or a business owner. This book is dedicated to all of you who take action and make project delivery easier and better for construction today.

TABLE OF CONTENTS

FOREWORD

When Felipe first approached me in 2016 to learn more about Scrum and to earn the ScrumMaster® certification, I was thrilled, as he was the first construction professional eager to explore how he could increase his capacity and overall productivity using the Scrum framework.

As the co-creator of Scrum and CEO of Scrum Inc., I continue to share best Scrum practices with organizations around the globe. I have witnessed how the framework has evolved over the years to meet the needs of many businesses in many industries. I have written extensively on Scrum rules and methods. Today, I am honoured to contribute the foreword to this book, which is the first of its kind for the construction industry.

The methodology I developed in 1993 and formalized in 1995 with Ken Schwaber has been adopted by the vast majority of software development companies around the world. And Ken and I soon realized that the benefits of Scrum are not limited to software and product development. Scrum proved especially effective in iterative and incremental knowledge transfer.

Many industries which involve complex work processes, such as education, manufacturing, research, science, finance, design and construction have since embraced and implemented Scrum in their organizations. It is widely used for products, services, and management tasks.

To help teams implement Scrum, we have developed the Scrum patterns. Scrum patterns are powerful tools to transform any organization and the output that team members will generate. There are over 200 patterns to choose from. They are the rules of the game outlined in the Scrum guide. Many teams in construction want to reap the benefits of Scrum but don't know how to play the game. Wanting it and embracing to implement it are two very different stories. People need to be willing to give up and let go of what they used to do. They need to embrace change. This game requires a set of skills and values including courage, trust, respect, transparency, and emotional intelligence.

Scrum patterns have been successful in a variety of organizations across different industries, which typically process significant amounts of data. We wanted to provide people with a blueprint that they can pick up to solve a specific problem over and over again.

Today, we mainly focus on the patterns that increase team performance. Two very powerful patterns to create impactful goals and to increase capacity are Pattern 71 (The Sprint Goal) and Pattern 80 (Good Housekeeping), which are both described in detail in Part II of this book. Regardless if you are new to Scrum or have been using the framework for years, these patterns are useful to review on a regular basis.

With Felipe's partnership in Scrum Inc, a new Scrum team focusing on Scrum in construction was formed to serve the millions of men and women working to build our world. His generous contributions to this team and the growing community of Scrum practitioners continue to have an outstanding impact on transforming people's work and lives.

This book aims at helping people across the construction industry to start using Scrum without asking permission. The stories bring to life how team leaders and frontline workers can begin to become more productive at work and achieve better project outcomes for themselves and others.

It's a book that encourages construction teams to take action and make project delivery easier and better for the industry today and in the future. The book focuses on empirical process control theory, which means that we learn by doing things hands-on with all our senses involved. Our actions and work are visible. The team is self-organized, self-motivated, and self-disciplined. In other words, Scrum is an iterative experimentation framework cycle which focuses on learning by doing. As a by-product, people reclaim their power, their freedom, and the joy of accomplishing great things. They simply have more fun doing what they do while getting done twice as much in half the time. And who wouldn't want this?

With this book, Felipe is showing the way for construction in the future. His vision to bust the myths and assumptions around Scrum and to simplify the life of construction project managers, superintendents, field engineers, and craft professionals, is unfolding.

If you work in the construction industry and are ready to embrace change and the opportunities that come with it, I encourage you to read this book.

Jeff Sutherland

Founder and Chairman at Scrum Inc.

Inventor and Co-creator of Scrum

Co-authored the bestselling book

Scrum: The Art of Doing Twice the Work in Half the Time

INTRODUCTION

WARNING

Use of any portions of these principles and methods will result in increased capacity. More time to improve, optimize, and coach others will be YOUR challenge. If you are completely satisfied with your capacity, read no further.

Congratulations! You are about to join millions of Scrum practitioners from around the world. This book is organized in three parts to get you started from exactly where you are now.

Part one is a series of stories that illustrate how Scrum works in design and construction. Part two is my Scrum story including chapters for the values and pillars making project delivery with Scrum easier, better, and faster. Part three is an invitation to create your own playbook with my insights and commentary for design and construction professionals to start using Scrum individually or with a team.

The singular purpose of this book is to enable you to shift from reading about Scrum to being a Scrum practitioner. Start from where you are, put up no barriers to beginning in your own way. The framework will propel you to sustained improvements that cascade across organizations and projects. To start, I encourage you to invest half an hour and read the current Scrum Guide online available for free in over 30 languages.

Scrum Guides: Home

Scrum Inc. is my personal provider of choice for education, resources, and support to practitioners of Scrum and Agile. This organization has helped professionals with resources, training, and consultation services in over 29 countries across six continents. By the end of 2020, Scrum

Inc. partnered with me to deliver design and construction Scrum training for practitioners worldwide. Read the guide to understand how the framework has inspired individuals, leaders, and organizations with practices, principles, and values that create workplaces that are joyful, prosperous, and sustainable.

By starting and practicing Scrum, you will be joining thousands of other construction professionals that repeatedly improve their work and simultaneously increase their creative freedom to develop and grow. You have my permission to learn, experiment, and repeat for greater customer value delivery individually, in teams, organizations, and our industry at large.

The benefits are both measurable and phenomenal.

Scrum transformed much more than my work. It improved my professional life, my private life, and my health. This lightweight system makes daily improvement a habit and builds an ever-increasing capacity. After adopting Scrum, individuals, and teams often immediately double, triple, and continue to iterate upon improvements driving team output beyond quadruple value delivery. The most impressive results I see are in capacity increase to better control schedules and the opportunity of daily self-development. Today, I continue to use the Scrum framework to onboard construction professionals in my organization and across the construction industry on four continents and counting.

While I studied electrical engineering at the University of Illinois at Chicago, I started working as an intern for an international general contractor on a traditional project management path that included "doing your time" to earn experiences and opportunities in the building industry with deep roots and dogmatic traditions.

Phrases like the ones below were not just memes you'd come across in social media feeds, they were daily mantras used by professionals to onboard newcomers into how buildings are constructed:

- This is the way we have always done it.

- Do it my way or there's the door.

- If it ain't broke, don't fix it.

- We are not reinventing the wheel here, just do your job.

- Put your head down and work hard.

- We are paid to do, not to think.

- Keep yourself busy, we reward hard work.

- We have traditions for good reasons.

- You don't have enough experience to improve _____ (insert any process here), just follow _____ (insert any long-term employee's name here) lead.

I quietly worked nearly a decade before waking up to the possibility that working longer and harder wasn't the only way to achieve beneficial results and deliver customer value. By luck, I happened to be attending a company seminar, drinking enough coffee to stay awake after working over 60 hours by midweek, to hear from a project director expounding on the benefits of adopting lean manufacturing principles to construction. The message was clear, there are more effective ways to work that don't require heroic effort or perfect luck. I asked the director how I could get started. He said it was as easy as reading a book and joining a small group of likeminded builders on a monthly conference call. I told him I was already working over 100 hours per week and didn't have time to read a book. He replied, "No problem, keep doing the same thing, and think about if you are being effective at work or being present at home." This wakeup call made me read *Lean Thinking: Banish Waste and Create Wealth in Your Corporation* by James P. Womack and Daniel T. Jones. Afterward, I earned my spot at the very next lean team meeting and have been practicing lean for over a decade.

Even with the priceless book knowledge and rich dialogue with numerous other leanminded partners, I struggled against my own habits and project obligations for months. I re-read, tested ideas, applied parts and what I thought applied to my work, and it paid off. I dramatically reduced my hours by more than 40 to consistently maintain a steady 60+ hours work week while still meeting all of my duties as an assistant manager and project lead with a handful of direct reports. At home, my wife was impressed with my newfound time and encouraged me to improve my skills and develop to even greater effectiveness. Applying lean helped me increase my capacity by a full work week. More importantly, I began upon a path of continuous learning and experimentation with lean in construction.

My development included continued book learning and on-the-job value experimentation by a stroke of fortune in 2014, I was recommended *Scrum: The art of doing twice the work in half the time* by Jeff Sutherland. I couldn't put the book down and finished reading it in three days. Immediately testing the framework with the help of my then toddler-aged son. Our Scrum team of two planned and completed our first team sprint that weekend. Our goal was to make packing for a vacation fun while enjoying indoor and outdoor playtime, exercise, and lunch. We met our Scrum goal, exceeded our planned activities, and had fun moving sticky notes across our makeshift Scrum board, a bedroom door. Originally, we thought there was no way we'd each be completely satisfied with each

Construction Scrum Case Studies

task's duration and quality but using the framework shattered both of our low expectations. This was so new and cool I had to try it out at work. Read more about my start with Scrum and some expanded Construction Scrum case studies using the link below.

That Sunday, I set up a board and became my own Product Owner, Scrum Master, and first Development Team member the following Monday. I doubled my output in the first couple of weeks and made applying lean principles a daily habit. My work hours decreased to between 50-60 per week total while my output continued to exponentially increase. More importantly, I freed up time to gain sufficient experiences to empower myself and earn a project manager promotion while simultaneously leading and contributing to multiple committees and still completing every available company training during working hours! A year later, I was approached by senior leadership to pilot a formal lean implementation on my current assignment and help onboard others in my region. Shortly afterward our lean pilot projects were helping other partners in two other regions. My output continued to improve and I started exploring the Lean Construction Institute's learning opportunities and growing my network of lean practitioners. Our pilot shared successes and challenges. Our team's efforts were positively recognized by our field crews, project leads, owner's representatives, trade partners, and sparked many other project teams to implement lean on their projects. Management took notice and a national position was created for a dedicated lean instigator.

I credit Scrum as the differentiator that enabled me to sustainably build my capacity far beyond what I thought possible.

Less than two years later, I would be standing in a multinational software company's meeting room in Palo Alto, California, not ten feet away from the co-creator of Scrum and the person I deemed most responsible for inspiring me to change my habits, Dr. Jeff Sutherland. He was leading me and a dozen others working to earn the ScrumMaster® certification. By then I had years of weekly sprints moved to 'Done', and Jeff was as excited to meet me as I was to meet him. I was his first construction professional using the framework. It was an amazing experience that led me to not only be a user of Scrum but also become a construction Scrum Master. In that capacity, I guided fellow construction professionals using Scrum to teach Scrum via interactive learning to thousands of industry partners from students to superintendents, admins to architects, engineers to executives, and industry professionals across hundreds of organizations. Jeff and his family even use Scrum for getting things done at home. I later used Scrum to organize my learning and teams to successfully earn an MBA from California State University at San Bernardino in 18 months without interrupting my business travel obligations, conference presentations, and work with the Lean Construction Institute.

In late 2019, the Lean Construction Institute asked me to satisfy the growing demand for Scrum by developing and coaching industry professionals through an introductory Scrum course at the Design Forum, Annual Congress, and for local Lean Communities of Practice. In the summer of 2020, I got a call from Scrum Inc. to share my Scrum application experiences in the design and construction industry. This led to a deep collaboration with Scrum Inc. earning me the privilege to be an official Scrum Trainer recognized by Dr. Jeff Sutherland. With each new Sprint, I continue sharing and inspiring others to work faster, with less effort, and with much more fun.

Today, I am a proud

- Author

- Board Member

- International Lean Construction Keynote Speaker & Podcast Host (https://www.theebfcshow.com)

- Entrepreneur

- MBA Graduate & Project Management Professional (PMP®)

- Scrum Master | Product Owner | Scrum@Scale Practitioner

- Researcher

1

THIS IS THE WAY WE HAVE ALWAYS DONE IT

Chapter 1

This is the way we have always done it.

I'm startled by the alarm clock going off at 4 am.

"What day is it?"

I grab my phone, squint in the dark at the bright screen, and see it's already Monday. The weekend passed in a flash, as usual when I was working at the job site. Saturday, I watched the middle school's steel frame come together on the main gymnasium, and Sunday I caught up on emails and subcontractor change order paperwork. There is no time to snooze today or the Los Angeles traffic will own me. My boss's voice is still ringing in my ears,

"Don't be late Jordan, you are leading the safety meeting Monday and you have to open the site, Mike is on vacation until Wednesday."

I jump into my clothes, skip breakfast, grab a Rockstar energy drink for the road, and leave the apartment in the same darkness I saw when I went to bed.

Traffic is light at 4:30 am. Surprisingly, I'm not the only early bird on the road. It's only 40ish miles from my place to the site on the interstate but then I'm on side streets for the last 20 minutes to the front gate. The project is a ten-acre site right in the middle of eastern Los Angeles county. It's just a bit smaller than ten adjacent football fields in a two-wide by five-long pattern extending about two city blocks.

Samantha's truck isn't in the lot yet but maybe she's bringing us donuts today since it is going to be a long day of meetings. She's a solid project manager and a third or fourth generation builder. Her dad was in the army. He was a carpentry and masonry specialist which means Samantha didn't fall far from the tree with her all-around builder know-how. She spent her high school and college years helping him with his residential framing construction company working outside all around southeastern California from Lake Havasu to Palm Springs. She could have been a superintendent but instead got her construction management degree and worked her way up the project management ladder at Solid Builders Inc over the last ten years.

The construction world is small, seems like everyone knows everyone or is at worst, second cousins. Samantha's dad is the reason I got this job. His company built an addition on my uncle's house when I was about to graduate as a construction manager from California State University Fresno and was striking out at career fairs. Jacob put me in touch with his daughter and we immediately connected over being only children and first-time college graduates coincidentally from the same school. Mike, our superintendent, is about a decade older than Smanatha's dad and came up through the carpenter's union working mostly in Los Angeles for a large multi-state commercial interior framing subcontractor. I don't think Mike knows Samantha's dad did carpentry in the army, he is shockingly introverted for being a superintendent, but he gets along with the field foremen well. He is well known in the area for being a part of some high-profile jobs such as the LA Rams Stadium. Our $50 million dollar school project is like the size of a small change order for Mike. After COVID-19, Mike decided to postpone retirement and end his career building smaller projects where he could mentor the next generation of builders.

Eventually, I get the gate opened.

"Good morning and buenos dias!" I greet the incoming crews

At 6:45 am, I start the safety talk with about 100 tradespeople. I share the dangers of working in confined spaces following the scheduled company safety bulletins.

Samantha doesn't disappoint and has donuts waiting for us in the conference room to munch on during our staff meeting. Caroline, our administrative assistant, gives us an unsolicited lecture about how all the sugar we eat is going to make our blood acidic and lead to premature aging. Eddie, our project coordinator, looks up from his laptop and slides another donut between his keyboard and cold brew coffee.

"Where is Victor?" I ask Samantha.

"He's watching the cement trucks like a hawk to make sure they clean off onsite before flying back on the road. We got a citation from the city for mud on the streets from the last pour."

I wonder why we are still placing concrete when the schedule said it should have been 100% done a month ago. Victor is second in command to Mike, as the assistant superintendent, he is focused on pushing schedule and keeping safety a daily priority.

We go through two hours of staff meeting minutes filled with discussing the open issues log, outstanding submittals, requests for information, and change orders. Victor makes it in time for the closing schedule review.

"We are almost on schedule since the steel crew started working overtime two weeks ago."

Samantha asks Eddie to email our scheduler, to get an updated eight-week look ahead schedule and forecast to project completion.

"We will need to submit a recovery schedule next month or it could delay our progress billing," Jessica, the project owner's representative, warns us.

While the others go to review the steel subcontract and prepare a draft letter to notify them of a potential delay, Samantha asks me to stay back.

"Brett stopped by on Saturday and told me how this job was bought with razor-thin margins taken only to keep his key guys working until some bigger jobs let loose in the city," I tell her what I had learned from Brett.

"Brett's a big boy and knows that our subcontract includes liquidated damages if this school doesn't open on time next fall. It's not personal Jordan, it's construction. Make sure Eddie gets the schedule update before the owner's meeting this afternoon. I don't need Jessica to remind me how lucky we are that the school pays on time each month despite being late on the last steel milestone. Mike picked the perfect time to be on vacation, we have been working twelve plus hours a day for months, most crews are working ten-hour shifts, and we haven't made up a single day."

Eddie strikes out with getting the schedule update in time and Jessica comes to the meeting with a detailed analysis of our last month's schedule update.

"I spoke to Brett last week and Solid Oak squeezed him during buyout so he can't staff this job with enough welders to keep up with the delivery schedule. We need more manpower. Our progress payment will be on hold until manpower and work progress meets the approved schedule dates," Jessica conveys the bad news."

When I ask Samantha about Jessica's response to our schedule after the meeting, she replies:

"When projects get behind, we have to push and add more people, 'this is the way we have always done it."

"Why did Mike allow the framing subcontractor to deliver the exterior studs early which caused the site logistics plan to change?"

I know that Brett got pretty heated about that with Mike because it forced him to use a bigger crane since he lost access to a third of two adjacent buildings he had planned to erect with smaller equipment.

"We have to support each other. I pushed Mike to accept the material to avoid escalation costs, and Brett owns 'means and methods' to install his work."

I remind Samantha that the contract schedule and initial site logistics plan didn't include losing so much area for stored materials.

"It's better to have long lead items onsite than be waiting for them to show up when you need them most," Samantha replies.

Her phone rings, it's our project scheduler, and her face says the day just got worse.

Back in my office, I check my calendar and see it is five minutes until my quarterly project engineer training starts. We used to have to drive in for a whole day and do these in person a few times a year before COVID. Now we have more sessions but only for an hour or two per quarter. Most of the time I practice my multitasking skills and listen in while catching up on email. I click the invite and I'm in. Pedro and Mia, project engineer training champions, are leading this session and the opening slide looks like a photo of a bunch of handwritten sticky notes on a whiteboard. They have my attention and I snap a screenshot of it for proof to Eddie how we can use PowerPoint to document our project progress.

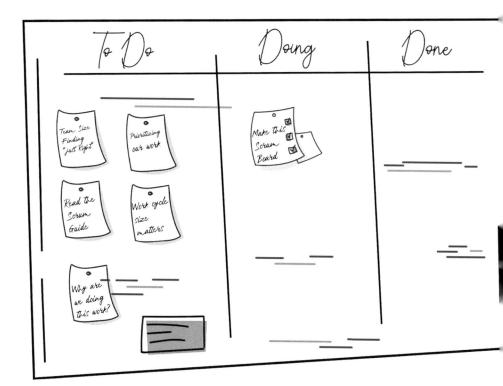

Figure 1.1

Two hours fly by before Samantha is at my door with the last donut. I'm excited to get it and share what I learned. Samantha always encourages the team to keep learning about how to be better builders, and this training was all about building teams that build faster every week they work with less effort.

"Everything that Mia and Pedro shared is free and there are many more free online resources available," I told her with excitement. "Pedro mentioned that they learned about this at last year's Lean Construction Institute virtual conference where they met dozens of architects, engineers, managers, and Lean practitioners getting Scrum certifications. I also heard that Solid Oak is looking into getting some people certified."

Eddie hears me getting excited about PowerPoint and comes over to join the conversation. I explain that they split the 25 of us into random teams of five, gave us a few instructions, a link to an online video and PDF to read and we had to make the opening slide using digital sticky notes on our digital collaboration whiteboards.

I am about to show them my notes when I remember Samantha's face when she walked over.

"How was your call about our schedule?"

"Well, the information Mike put in the schedule update shows we are about six weeks behind and we'll need to increase crew sizes for the mechanical, electrical, plumbing, and finish trades next quarter during the final summer building rush when the union halls are the most empty. Solid Oak's executives got the schedule naughty list and we are at the top. I think that we are getting a visit this week from Solid Oak's leadership team."

"Guys, listen, this training I watched today included case studies of construction projects finishing ahead of schedule without adding extra people using this system they call Scrum," I explain.

"How is rugby going to help?" Eddie is bright and direct as usual.

"Let's grab lunch in the conference room and hear Jordan out," Sam suggests.

We eat and I start talking about what I have learned.

"Mia and Pedro said that they even used Scrum to prepare for the training and lead the session. They both started using it personally on their medical office building project for months, and people kept asking them about their sticky notes so much they decided to share it at the next training session. Their project manager hadn't adopted it but also wasn't discouraging them."

Samantha shoots me a look. Caroline joins us as I finish sketching this

To Do   *Doing*   *Done*

Scrum board on the conference room whiteboard.

"Scrum, that's a software management thing. My kids use that at the video-sharing social network company up in San Francisco. I see their Scrum boards in their home offices when we video chat on the weekends with lots of colored sticky notes."

Caroline doesn't ever disappoint with her pop culture trivia knowledge base.

"Pedro and Mia showed us a few pictures of Scrum boards from the conference training and the common theme was that they all had at least three columns labeled like the one I just drew," I keep talking.

"My kids explained that the sticky notes represent items of work and that people actually move them around as they change state, one by one." Caroline adds her two cents to the conversation.

"Mia said it is super easy to get started. People really work on tasks one thing at a time and that she learned multitasking actually makes you slower," I explain "Can you make stickies in digital formats, or does it have to be paper and marker?" Eddie wants to know.

"That got asked in the training, and Pedro said the better practice is to start simple before digitizing so you learn the process first and then adapt in software tools if you aren't co-located."

Victor returns with today's lunch truck special, tacos, and an energy drink in his hands "Don't stop because I'm here." Victor isn't shy about being curious, and I keep going.

"They used Scrum to teach us about prioritization, work cycles, goals, and team size. Pedro and Mia showed us how they took their project's issues list and wrote it out as sticky notes on their Scrum board."

"Well, that's not lean, that is wasted effort. Even I know you can move cells around on spreadsheets," Victor replies.

"Pedro explained that the spreadsheet is always shared onscreen or printed out so it seemed like only the owner of the sheet could move stuff. In minutes of putting the same things on a Scrum board, their superintendent and project manager debated and then agreed on what needed to be done first, second, third, and last. They showed us before and after pictures, some items even got taken off the list. The superintendent decided the fieldwork priorities, and their manager decided the office ones but then they had to negotiate on interconnected tasks. This is the "Backlog" list, and the person who has the ultimate responsibility for what the team delivers to the client is the owner of the list and has the final say on the order. In Scrum, they call this person the Product Owner."

"That's you, Samantha, you own the responsibility for this project contrary to what Mike tells us out there. I know who signs off on his performance evaluation," Victor interrupts me.

"Correction, we together own this project's success, Victor, but I know what you mean. My neck is on the line for every profit projection. Jerry and Larry are crystal clear on that." Samantha replies.

She also bought the job out and negotiated all the contracts. She let me help her coordinate the scopes before we mobilized onsite last year.

"The next thing we learned is that size matters," I keep sharing my newly acquired wisdom.

Eddie nearly spits out his Cuban sandwich, and I actually blush while I say, "Work cycles, work cycle size matters. Mia showed us how. She and Pedro plan their submittals, coordination, and engineering work in weekly cycles. They said this allows for consistent feedback and they can gauge how much is planned and done in a week's time frame. They also said this is called a Sprint but you don't have to run ragged to be fast. They actually shared how they tracked their progress and started getting so much done that they could spend more time in the field learning from the foremen how the building actually comes together while still getting their trade management work completed each day."

"That's great for engineers but how does watching others work help their project?"

Victor is paying attention as usual and reminds me of the next point.

"Pedro said that our projects are all about what we build for the eventual customers or building users, medical patients for this job, and students for ours. The goal of a completed building can be broken down into smaller goals that when achieved make progress towards the larger end goal."

"Sounds a little like schedule milestones," Victor throws in.

"That's pretty close but Mia said schedule milestones separate the end of one project phase from the start of another. Goals in Scrum give the team the answer to "why" this phase of work is important and informs the "what" we need to do to achieve it. Each week they come up with a Sprint Goal that helps them decide what must be done and helps them focus on delivering value that makes building progress."

Samantha looks at Victor: "A goal Mike left us before leaving on vacation was to get from 98% done with concrete operations to 100% before he comes back."

Victor points out the conference room window to the piles and piles of exterior metal studs: "If that was true, we shouldn't have accepted all the exterior metal studs onsite four months early. It choked the steel installation and made the concrete crews have to run pump trucks and lines halfway across the site instead of by adjacent placement with chutes."

"My kids put their Scrum goal right on the whiteboard so they all see it," Caroline adds.

I share the picture of Pedro and Mia's Scrum board for the class with the goal to 'Understand what Scrum is and how to use it.'

Eddie turns to Samantha: "Wasn't the early stud delivery done to head off the rising metal costs that the framer excluded from his contract?"

"Exactly," Samanta replies, "We didn't include escalation or we risked not winning the bid, and since the site was wide open, it seemed like the right call at the time. We talked about it at the staff meeting for weeks."

Victor shoots back at Samantha: "Mike and I were jumping all over the site splitting time between steel and concrete, we didn't get a vote on the studs."

That reminds me of the second to last part of the training: teams.

"Mia said one of the keys to good Scrum is that work is done in small teams, groups of three to nine, typically. The team has to have all the necessary skills to do the work needed to achieve the Sprint Goal. Titles don't matter as much as skills and cross-functional teams decide how much work they can do in a given work cycle."

"Scrum is definitely not the way we have always done it in construction," Samantha is smiling, and so is Victor.

"I agreed to start using Scrum at the end of the training. Here is my first Scrum board." I show them my tablet screen.

"Don't laugh, Eddie, yes it is a spreadsheet. Everyone made a Scrum

To Do	Doing	Done
Set a goal for the week. Plan tomorrow's work.	Read the Scrum Guide.	Attend the PE training webinar. Lead Monday safety huddle.

Table 1.1

board during the breakout exercises. Some used whiteboards and sticky notes while others used software."

"I'll be the first to admit it won't be in any case studies but I did get two things done today." Eddie laughs. "Do meetings count? Because if they do, I got two more things done than you."

I explain how each task has to deliver value for the customer or the next person receiving your work. Learning is part of becoming more cross-functional and Pedro said he and Mia counted training as value-added. I share a bit more about the case studies before we have to clear the room for the foremen meeting.

"That sounds like some training Jordan, when does the field get their turn?" Victor wants to know.

"Sounds like we all just got it, we've been in here for two hours," Eddie laughs.

After the foremen meeting, Samantha and I regroup to call Brett about manpower in her office. Samantha shares with him what our goal is for this week and asks him what he thinks is possible. We talked for an hour and didn't even mention sending him a delay letter. After a pause, so long I thought the phone disconnected, Brett offers to pull some people from the boltup crew to the raising crews so that we'll get ahead of the beam deliveries and show Jessica progress outside her office window. Samantha sends me out to the field to let Victor know about our new agreement with Brett.

When I open the trailer door to come back in, I find Samantha talking with Caroline about Scrum and they both turn and smile at me.

"Are there donut crumbs on my face again?"

"No, but you got us stirred up about Scrum." Caroline admits, "And you have a stain on your collar but I wasn't going to say anything."

Samantha interrupts: "I called Pedro and Mia's manager. Since they started using Scrum, those two haven't missed a critical submittal or had a request for information get old enough on the weekly report to warrant discussion with the architect during the owner's meeting. Andrew doesn't give all the credit to Scrum, they are talented project engineers, but he says they are on top of their work and have respect from the field leader, too. I was so shocked by the last phone call with Brett that I had to meet him in person to make sure it was real."

We talk about the schedule and agree that if we keep going without changing, Jessica is going to rightfully hold our progress payment.

The next morning, my alarm clock starts going off with musical chimes at 4 am as usual.

What is Mike going to do when he finds out that Brett's crews are no longer working overtime?

I grab my phone and see a text from Samantha, she must have been thinking the same thing. I rub my eyes to adjust to the bright screen of my mobile and read that she's bringing in Mike's favorite croissants this morning at 7 am.

It's already Wednesday, yesterday flew by as many days before. It was after 7 pm until we finally closed the trailer. Samantha, Eddie, and I went over the spreadsheet issues list and meeting calendar to convert the important stuff to sticky notes and delete the rest. We used the updated schedule report from Tony to craft three goals, one for each of the next three weeks based on the most critical fieldwork that gets steel and concrete done-done. I never understood why things can't just be 'done' but Samantha said to give it a few more years and I would know what 'done-done' means. We all talked and Eddie made us laugh as usual too. Samantha gave us context for what was stove-hot versus backburner-cold. We prioritized and moved tags around on a corner of the conference room whiteboard into four columns. Stove-hot tags were at the top of the list and important, backburner-hot tags were at the bottom. We agreed to make the column of notes closest to the 'Doing' column fire-hot priority and columns towards the left less hot. Eddie was going to make the goals more fancy looking in PowerPoint and print

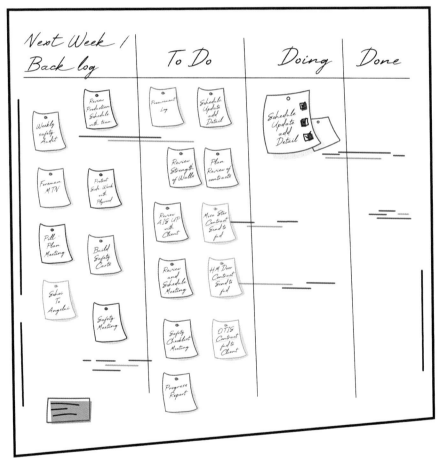

Figure 1.2

them out in the morning after the daily safety orientation meeting.

It wasn't perfect but the three of us now knew exactly why and what was going to happen and by whom. That was worth staying late, and Samantha did feed us pizza.

As I drive into the site this Wednesday morning, the middle school's steel frame is still invisible but the adjacent street lights are bright enough for me to see all the columns are up pointing into the sky. Everyone can tell this is going to be a gymnasium soon. I see Mike's office light shining onto the parking lot. He usually beats us all in being the first on-site, and today, his first day back from vacation is no exception. I quickly inhale the last of my energy drink and walk in.

"Jordan, I see there has been some sticky note wallpapering since I've been gone. How did Brett's crew do on Saturday?"

"Good morning to you, too, Mike," I reply. "They got the last two corners in before the first break and got all the roof trusses set before leaving at 3:30 pm."

"That does warrant a good morning, kid. I told you Brett just needed the right amount of pressure to motivate his crews."

I share with Mike all about the owner's meeting, schedule update delay, and Samantha's call with Brett. Before I can mention Scrum, his phone starts going off, and out of the trailer, he goes.

Eddie enters a few minutes later and asks if anyone has shown up for the safety orientation.

"You have three big customers today," he smiles and disappears around the corner to the conference room.

Samantha arrives just after Caroline gets settled in at the front desk. She is carrying a few pink boxes of buttery goodness that instantly raise my hopes and stir up some hunger pangs.

"Please give me a hand, Jordan, I've got a few more boxes in my truck."

Samantha explains her plan to share with Mike some of the changes we made while she delivers some extra boxes to Jessica and her staff for goodwill before we meet later this afternoon to discuss change orders and probably schedule. She tells me that 'hangry' people have 'no' saying superpowers and that this is a trick she learned from her dad.

The next few days are peacefully quiet compared to the nearly endless phone calls last week about schedule and manpower. Mike isn't convinced that sticky notes are going to produce the needed manpower and overtime to get the job done but he likes the ability to see his request for us making progress on the conference room whiteboard.

"Hey Samantha, I am not worried about the leadership's opinion about our project. As long as we are being proactive we have nothing to worry about. I had a meeting with our scheduler on Friday to go over a few recovery schedule scenarios so we can have something in Jessica's hands by Monday. Once the interiors start, we'll be able to go split shifts and easily make up the time later this year. I have done it a thousand times."

"The labor market isn't what it was in the past, and union business agents have been saying there's no one sitting at home on the bench waiting to be called into work even before COVID started," Victor reminds us "We'll see Victor, I have some favors to call in before I start believing that people aren't available for good work. At the stadium, people came out of retirement to work the night shift."

"This is a middle school, Mike. How many times have we been interviewed by the press about it?"

A couple of months later, I take Eddie on a field trip to see Pedro and Mia's job. They are hosting us to share more about what they've recently been learning about Scrum and mostly to give us a chance to ask questions and see examples.

We start with a tour of their medical office building project, which is stunningly clean.

Every time we see tradespeople, they wave to our hosts and smile.

"Wow, this is amazing! When I see the trades on our site, I get eye rolls and 'hey intern' comments," Eddie remarks.

Mia turns around: "Yeah, I remember those days. We've been with some of these crews for over a year and since we're out here so much, we pretty much know everyone by first name."

"We realized before using Scrum, it was a question of us versus them and now we acknowledge that we're all on the same team," Pedro explains.

Back in the trailer we see pull planning boards and Scrum boards in most offices. The conference room even has a Scrum board for constraint tracking.

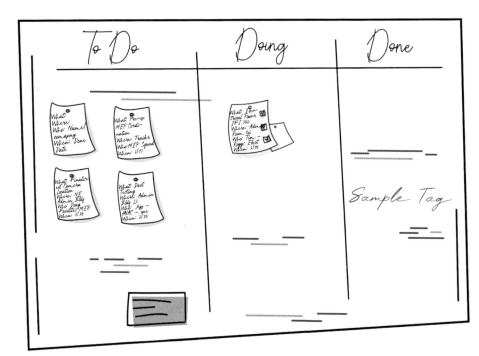

Figure 1.3

"Wow!" I blurt out loud, "You got the subs to use Scrum."

Pedro laughs and explains that they call them trade partners, not subs. He tells us that he and Mia learned about the difference between the two words when listening to episodes of The EBFC Show podcast.

"That's got to be a construction podcast because we love acronyms in construction."

"That's right Eddie," Mia explains, "it features people working around the world making construction easier, better, and faster. We have lots of wheel time driving in LA to work, so Pedro and I listen to audiobooks and podcasts in the car and try what we learn on-site."

"Do they have shows on Scrum?" I want to know.

"Yep, Jordan, they have a Scrum playlist on YouTube."

Pedro goes on to tell us about some of the case studies shared on the show that inspired them to try marrying pull planning and Scrum. He gives us a link to this show to check out after we take a bunch of pictures and get our fill of questions.

Scrum Elevating Construction with Jason Schroeder

"What about Danny, your superintendent, does he do Scrum? He doesn't seem to have a board in his office."

I want to fist bump Eddie for asking this before we leave. Thinking of Mike on our job, I realize that after two months, his initial support level hasn't gone up. He still definitely adds to our planning sessions and adds tags for us on the Scrum board, but he isn't doing it himself.

Pedro and Mia both laugh.

"Danny doesn't need to make tags, he runs the project." Mia replies.

And Pedro keeps going: "Danny used to say that when we first started. He usually has the whole conference room full of sticky notes and boards made by the foremen. He says that the pull planning boards are his

Scrum board and that we are his best constraint removal Scrum team."

"What's the difference between pull planning and Scrum?" I want to know.

"Check out the podcast, it isn't either one or the other," Mia suggests.

I admit that I've never seen pull planning and we've only been doing Scrum long enough to have seven Sprints under our 'Done' column. They see us off and we have plans to be back next week. We leave after 3 pm and traffic back to our job is bad enough for Eddie and me to listen to one podcast episode and a live stream recording of Scrum and Last Planner System.

Dr. Jeff Sutherland and Scrum Inc. Principal, Dee Rhoda
Scrum in Construction

Lucien Zoll and Felipe Engineer-Manriquez
Scrum in Design and Construction AMA Live Stream

Chapter 2

Do it my way or there's the door

The sign in the kitchen says: "Take Some - Make Some. You just finished the last cup."

Nancy is well organized, but also equally strict with how things run in the field office. She didn't get to be Bill's lifelong assistant by letting people ignore standards or slip on personal accountability. Bill, the general superintendent with Bur Oak Builders, will likely end his career with the completion of this three-year exterior renovation and interior condominium build-out project in the very busy business district of Chicago.

"Hey Nancy, you are right, but I didn't finish making my cup yet. It still needs cream and sugar."

"I don't know how you can drink so much coffee with sugar and stay so thin," Nancy gives the senior project manager a dutiful polite smile.

"It's because I have a great collection of jeans. They're all the same size, so when one pair gets tight, I skip dinner so tomorrow's pair fits just right."

Kevin is best friends with William, the Project Executive, and keeps reminding everyone daily that the two of them vacation together and hang out every weekend. Kevin and William were roommates during college and Nancy thinks William is loyal to a fault.

Bur Oak Builders is family-owned and operated. Three Tyler generations have led the organization from multi-family residential in the 1960s to becoming the city's premier commercial, light industrial, and historical restoration general contractor of choice since 2000. Much of the business district work has included many of the city's historic places, such as Engine Company 129, Truck 50 at 8120 South Ashland Avenue, and many other of the city's most ornate buildings. The Tyler's pride themselves on being a part of the city's history and preserving it. William grew up on the Westside and went to school with a few of the Tyler brothers and eventually married Sheila Tyler, Liam's only daughter and Bur Oak's head of accounting. Bur Oak doesn't have many written policies but everyone knows you follow all of those from the president. Liam's motto is "Do it my way or there's the door." He is very selective on who can join the company and is the final interviewer for any hire at all levels. More than a few people find out which unwritten policies they violated when Liam dismisses them. Bill is Liam's uncle and has been a part of the company's success with historic renovations since the 1970s.

"I didn't make any coffee, it's already after 12, but I'll tell Gabriel to make some after the coordination meeting ends." Kevin walks past Nancy's desk with the last cup of coffee and the unwashed pot still in the machine.

Nancy frowns and texts Gabriel "Eight missed opportunities in March... Kevin took the last cup again." Gabriel is on a conference call with the project's architect and masonry consultant to address the historic landmark society's latest round of exterior facade comments. He glances at his phone and quickly sends back a flying dollar emoji to Nancy and a single tear face. If Kevin gets to 15 without at least one pot of coffee making, he'll owe Bill five dollars.

Gabriel is an experienced civil engineer and joined Bur Oak while working to earn his Masters. He wants to get the best experience with historic building construction before becoming a licensed structural engineer. Growing up in Cicero, he became obsessed with construction, seeing Chicago's skyline change from his backyard over the years as many masonry buildings got overshadowed with towers of glass. Even while in undergraduate studies, he'd get into arguments with architectural students about how less practical glass curtain wall buildings were as compared to the higher mass options of concrete, brick, block, terra cotta, and precast. His passion for traditional building styles and preservation

Meeting Minutes

Topic	Discussion	Responsible
Safety Inspections	Orientations are mandatory. Weekly reports are available on the shared drive	Alicia
Schedule	Multitasking is a myth. If you think you are good at it, read this sentence while simultaneously remembering the last time you drove, talked on the phone, and didn't miss your desired exit. People really work on tasks one at a time. Scrum promotes this flow enabling good practice every time you move a sticky note from the Doing to Done column after the task is complete. Dual-Task Interference or Context Switching describes the mental process of changing between tasks, tools, or projects. Gerald Weinberg wrote about this in his book, *Quality Software Management: Systems Thinking, back in 1991.* Gloria Mark, Professor, and Researcher at the University of California at Irvine, reports real-world research findings that support Gerald's earlier observations that people lose more than 20% of their time by mentally switching from one task/project/mode of action to another. She has several published papers on this topic which you can learn more about here at the University of California, Irvine.	
Cost	Change order log reviewed, no open change orders	Kevin

Table 2.1

quickly won Liam over during his assistant manager interview. "Tsk, tsk, tsk" Alicia shoots Gabriel a smile while she is typing "multi-tasking is a myth" on their shared meeting minutes document.

Gabriel smiles and puts his phone down before asking Karen, the project architect, to repeat herself because he missed the question she just asked him.

Alicia grew up on the south side of the city. She bucked the family tradition of working in the family restaurant business and instead studied hard in high school and put herself through state school on scholarships and student loans. She was the first of her family to graduate from college and maintained a disciplined habit of learning something new weekly. She likes to joke that she earned her minor in project management from YouTube university. Her favorite videos are typically about Agile project management.

Kevin's youngest brother works for a dot com in the downtown business district that uses Scrum for software development and he's told Alicia a few times that Scrum is more suited for designers who go on and on about their work being iterative and non-sequential. The last time they talked about it, he pointed to the project's monthly payment application and schedule.

"See that, Alicia? Construction projects are measured in months and years, and progress payments are received for work in place. We don't need Scrum or Kanban here. We need to stay on top of the contracts with the trades and hold them accountable to what they signed up for."

This week Kevin brings Alicia his college copy of the Project Management Institute's Project Management Body of Knowledge Guide (PMBOK).

"William got the project started. That was the Initiating phase. Bill worked on the master schedule, which is the Planning phase. We are in the Executing and the Monitoring and Controlling phases. You'll be part of the Closing phase when we finish commissioning and handover to the owner in two years."

Alicia already learned in college that construction projects are supposed to follow the five project management process groups:

- Initiating

- Planning

- Executing

- Monitoring and Controlling

- Closing

Project Management Institute Announces Acquisition of Disciplined Agile

She also remembered her professor sharing that in 2019, the Project Management Institute acquired Disciplined Agile and that many of the continuing education credits Certified Project Management Professionals earn are more and more about Agile and Scrum in particular.

Kevin's PMBOK is dated 1998 and Alicia decides to just let that fact stay on the cover of the guide rather than extend the one-way conversation. It is clear from Kevin's LinkedIn profile that he hasn't renewed his credential since then either.

Alicia is used to people telling her what isn't possible. She had decades of that growing up. As a passionate learner and avid student of history, she knows better. She remembers Nelson Mandela's words

"It always seems impossible until it's done."

Alicia smiles at Kevin and pushes the PMBOK back.

"Thanks, but I'll look online and check out the current guide."

"Sure, Alicia, but things haven't changed in construction."

"Alicia, why are you so intrigued by Scrum?"

Gabriel is making the last afternoon pot of coffee before their staff meeting.

"Our project is doing okay, why try to change it?"

Alicia hands Gabriel a clean coffee pot.

"I used to do payroll and procurement for my family's restaurants while going to school. If a customer didn't pay their bill before leaving, we'd have the cops there. If we didn't pay our suppliers, we'd have no deliveries. If we didn't pay our staff each week, no one would work and no customers would be served. Construction is a bit different in what people expect or really what we put up with."

Gabriel pours Alicia a cup of coffee before she continues.

"This $95 million dollar project started at $55 million and today has about $5 million in outstanding change orders with a large part of that being for already completed time and material change order work."

"How do you remember those numbers off the top of your head so well?"

Alicia frowns. "I get copied on all the back and forth emails from Kevin to the subcontractors and I draft the monthly reports for the project owner and the internal Bur Oak Building reports for Liam. I use my whiteboard as a Scrum board to keep track of the contracts and change orders."

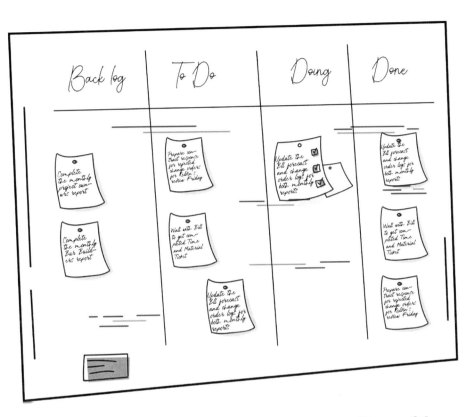

Figure 2.1

She takes Gabriel over to her office to see the Scrum board. Gabriel looks at the four columns labeled: Backlog, To Do, Doing, and Done.

"I see. What's the significance of the diamond tag about cash flow?"

"That's the main purpose or goal for my weekly work. Liam told me that Bur Oak Builders has only been able to survive all the economic recessions over the years due to having positive cash flows to keep us paid for the hard work we do. The same has been true for my family's restaurant business. The restaurants survive on more than just good food and friendly service, timely payment for services rendered factor in too."

"Gabriel, on my last job walk Bill told me that even the foremen are complaining about how their companies are financing the job."

Gabriel looks at the open change order value. "It looks like construction projects are subject to Newton's Laws of Motion, too."

Now it was Alicia who had a puzzled look on her face.

"You know, Newton's Third Law of Motion. For every action, there is an equal and opposite reaction. If our contractors aren't sure about when they'll be paid for their work, it makes it harder to plan manpower and supplies. Now that I see the numbers, it seems so obvious."

Alicia nods. "Exactly, that is what Scrum boards do, radiate information and enable the right amount of work to flow at the right place and at the right time. Just like in lean manufacturing, Agile teams use handwritten, drawn, printed, or digital displays to see the latest information at a glance. Making things visible helps to increase transparency, raise problems to the surface, and promote responsibility.

"It looks like Kevin and I are abiding by Newton's law. Every single time I talk about Scrum, he tries to convince me of why traditional project management is best for construction."

They both laugh. "I'm not actually trying to convince him to do Scrum. I haven't even tried to convince you, and we work together most of every day. Maybe Kevin thinks I am, since I talk about it so much."

Gabriel nods. "That explains the defensive tone of voice that he seems to keep reserved for you only."

"Well, William thinks it's cool and says I'm one of the only engineers that don't work on weekends to keep up."

Alicia's phone rings, it is Bill. "Gabriel, Bill's ready to meet me at the mechanical room and go over some new change order work. Let's talk more about this later."

Bill is writing in his notebook as usual while holding open the door to the roof-level mechanical room using his tablet as a writing surface.

"Good afternoon Bill, did Gabriel show you how to use your tablet to write notes."

Bill smiles, "Yes, several times. He even showed me how to charge the fancy pen. It runs out of battery power faster than a dollar pen runs out of ink."

"You have a good point there. How is it working out for the drawings?"

"Can't complain there, It Is lighter than carrying rolls of even half size sets of drawings sheets and the specs are searchable."

They walk through the mechanical room and Alicia takes some pictures of the existing boilers. The building used to be an office and was now going to house about ten residences per floor. The developer wanted the existing boilers to stay but now the designed new additions weren't going to fit.

"Alicia, I need a potential change order number to get a concrete x-ray technician here to see if these existing pipes have an elbow in the slab. The survey seems to indicate that they do and we won't be able to set the equipment pad using the designed layout."

"You got it, Bill. You know what they say, change is guaranteed." Alicia finishes taking some pictures to add to the files for this potential change.

She remembers that Scrum is best suited for complicated and complex work where linear prediction or simple models don't help make use of predictions for the work. By using small experiments or little batches of work, teams can inspect and adapt to pivot as needed while staying focused on delivering customer value.

She looks up the next potential change order number on her tablet.

"Bill, how did you know the pipe is likely to change direction in the slab?"

Bill points to his gray beard and says, "You don't get this much white hair by guessing right all the time. I've seen this before in buildings of about this age and blindly followed the drawings to the detriment of the whole project. These are 300-gallon units. If we punch a hole in the outlet pipe, there will be tens of thousands of dollars of damage when the water ruins all the finished work on the floors below."

"We are definitely facing uncertainty on this building, Bill. No as-built drawings and unpredictable scope changes every time we touch something that is supposed to remain in place."

Bill remembers something Alicia talked about when they first met.

"Isn't an Agile mindset all about responding to change? Well from my perspective, we often have to try something we think might work, see if it does or doesn't, and adjust our plans based on what we learn."

Alicia's face lights up, "Exactly Bill, you are 100% correct. Why do you think Kevin disagrees with Agile being good for construction?"

Bill closes his notebook and pauses for a long minute.

"From his perspective, this job looks and feels a lot like the last dozen he's been on. He's got a strong relationship with the owner and an even stronger one with William. His main responsibility is to manage the budget and the contracted time for this project's scope of work. From his view, everything is operating as normal."

Alicia pauses to let that sink in. She hadn't realized Kevin's experiences as a project manager. She assumed Kevin was seeing what she was seeing, lots of uncertainty, and frustrated workers. She thought about the last time he was in the building. It has been at least half a year.

They leave the mechanical room, and while they are heading to the roof, Bill shares a story about when he moved up from journeyman carpenter to foreman.

"In the old days, we had to just try and figure things out ourselves. Sometimes we were shown what to do by boing told what not to do. We didn't have online videos or smartphones either."

"Why didn't you become an executive and join Liam at the main office to lead more projects?" Alicia wanted to know. In her opinion, Bill was a natural teacher. .

"Look, Liam is a numbers guy and I am more of a people person. I see myself leading work in the field, not reading reports, going to meetings, or making staff decisions."

"Bill, why does Liam tell people, "Do it my way or there's the door" when he's firing people?".

He let out a belly laugh. "That's what his father often told him when he was training him to take over the business in the early 90s. Liam didn't want to work in the business. He studied finance in college and had plans of traveling before getting a full-time job. Liam senior threatened to cut him off if he didn't get right to work telling him he'd had plenty of fun while in college and now it was time to work. My brother was pragmatic, our business put many of us to work and kept our bellies full when many others from our neighborhood had to leave the city to find work to feed their families. Liam was a bit of a dreamer but he worked as hard in school learning about money and economics as I was concentrating on carpentry and general construction."

Alicia saw a bit of herself in Liam's story. Her father put pressure on her to just start working right after high school. She rebelled and went her own way. It made for a lot of awkward family dinners for a few years but her dad was proud of her. Her brothers teased her about her loans but she was independent and living on her own terms.

"So, Liam was just doing what he thought was best for the company like your brother taught him."

Bill nods, "There are a hundred families depending on our business to succeed for their income and dozens of building owners and countless more occupants that need us to do a top-quality job. As long as operations continue to enable that, Liam gets the message to keep things the same. Before my brother passed away, he told Liam how most proud he was of growing the Bur Oak Builders reputation in and beyond Chicago's city limits."

They stood on the roof overlooking the city, skyscrapers in all directions except East where Lake Michigan's calm waters glistened in the afternoon sunlight.

"I've worked with lots of project engineers over the years, Alicia. You are like three or four of the best ones rolled into one single person. Your work is always done well and I see you learning each day and sharing it with others. Have you ever thought about transitioning to the field? You have the right kind of people skills and self-organization."

Alicia is caught by surprise. They keep talking for a while longer before she goes back downstairs to the office. Bill is going to mention his observations to William on Friday and he is going to see Liam this weekend.

Alicia feels energized and thinks about a recent construction podcast video she saw featuring a superintendent addressing why people are resistant to trying new ways of working in construction. He mentioned that many of the skeptics were not aware of how the effort needed today has radically increased as compared to even ten years ago. If change is subtle and slow, people aren't likely to respond. She gets back to her office and checks her play history to watch this video again.

Why we need The Lean Builder | S2 The EBFC
Show 018 (clip)

When Alicia finishes the video, she realizes that some resistance to doing things differently was inside of her. She got feedback from Bill that confirmed that she was different and different in a good way. In order for her to be Agile, the entire organization wouldn't need to be. The team was supporting her development and providing conditions to test her evolving mindset. No one, not even Kevin, was stopping Alicia from practicing Scrum.

She didn't need to conform. Her journey was one of many doors to pass through.

Chapter 3

If it ain't broke, don't fix it

"Jay, your meeting with Hannah and Nathan is scheduled." Jay looks up from his email. Amber is standing in the doorway with her tablet.

"Does tomorrow morning still work best? You have to leave for the airport right after, or you'll miss your flight."

Jay nods., "Thank you, Amber, it will have to be tomorrow morning, as Peter will want to know how the meeting went before the weekly planning meeting next Monday."

Peter is the firm's founder. He is well known around the engineering world as meticulous and persistent. The firm's name, Bespoke Structural Engineering Solutions, matches Peter's approach. Jay started working for Peter right after college. Over the decades he earned design experience and how to achieve win-win construction project successes with owners, designers, and builders. Peter became more of a mentor than a boss over the years. Today, Jay is leading several teams of engineers in San Francisco and Phoenix. The California office has a full-time Agile coach dedicated to train teams on Scrum and oversee cross-functional team development to ensure effective outcomes for Bespoke Structural Engineering Solutions. Jay no longer wonders why Peter invests in Audrey's recommendations. She is an Agile Coach and her guidance with teams led to changes to their onboarding process that dramatically increased employee engagement and retention. Leadership is embracing the Scrum framework from Peter's level and down, and every team Audrey works with doubles their output while maintaining a steady workweek. Gone are the late nights and weekend work. Now Jay is in charge of implementing this approach in Phoenix this calendar year. So far, the Phoenix office hasn't started on any of Audrey's recommendations. Jay is going to visit the office leaders, Nathan and Hannah tomorrow.

The Phoenix office is experiencing a big growth spike. New projects for healthcare and data centers are testing Nathan's ability to find and hire local talent both from competing firms and college graduates. Hannah is still in need of two more engineers. Her teams are clocking six and seven-day work weeks since the start of the year with no end in sight. Avi is one of Hannah's best structural engineers and he has been in her office multiple times asking for help. His current projects would win records for long meetings durations. He has resorted to running calculations and detailing on his laptop during coordination meetings of the other projects which have caused some quality issues with his otherwise perfect work.

Jay checks his watch and glances out the window from the Phoenix office. The desert outside isn't as close as it used to be. Commercial buildings, houses, and shopping centers weave in and out from the busy roads. When this office became available a decade ago, the office was a stone's throw from the edges of the Sonoran Desert. Scrum also wasn't a word spoken inside engineering firms either in the early 2000s.

"Morning Jay, I'm sorry to keep you waiting. Nathan is wrapping up with a new client and will join us shortly. You know how short-staffed we are here. How was your flight?" Hannah, the Project Executive, interrupts his thoughts.

"My flight was uneventful. No matter how many times I do it, there is no way to prepare for the change in air-conditioned airport temperature to the 100+ degrees Phoenix heat. I'm staying all week so we can chat more later. Let's get started and I'll fill in Nathan afterward."

Forty-five minutes fly by. Jay shares the current business plan with Hannah including the implementation of Agile methods this year. Hannah doesn't seem very enthusiastic about this looming change. She and Nathan have grown the firm from a handful of staff to over two dozen engineers. Most of the new hires are replacing retiring engineers who worked for decades in the Phoenix office. The skills and experience gap are legitimate factors in their ability to grow and meet business demands. Jay acknowledges the problems and reminds Hannah that other firms are facing the same challenges.

"Hannah, we have to adapt or our clients will take their business to others that can keep up."

Nathan, the program director, joins with about 15 minutes left until the next meeting. He has just sold another job. The typical congratulations and smiles from Jay and Hannah don't last more than seconds due to the prior conversation. Finally, Jay gets up and goes to the whiteboard.

"I understand and agree that we can't add more to your plate, Nathan. Let's make one change to take some of the burden off your team. When I was growing up in engineering, people used to say, 'If it ain't broke, don't fix it.' Well, our methods aren't working, so let's all fix this."

At the whiteboard, Jay grabs a dry erase marker and writes a tall column of capital letters that spell 'DOWNTIME'.

D
O
W
N
T
I
M
E

When Audrey started with one of our hardest working teams, this is all they focused on for a month. We learned that DOWNTIME is everywhere and keeps us from doing what our customers need most, our work. Nathan speaks up first.

"Jay, we aren't wasting time on purpose, we need more people."

Jay nods and quickly writes out eight words.

"I was the team's project executive at the time, and I had to learn this too before we could learn about Scrum. Peter is very encouraging and committed to our development."

Defect

Overproduction

Waiting

Non-utilized talent

Transportation

Inventory

Motion

Excess processing

Jay pauses to let them read the list. Without any explanations, he hands them each a marker and asks them to pick the top three words that are affecting their operations right now.

"Don't overthink it and don't worry about being in agreement. Just pick the first three words that come to mind."

Defect ✓

Overproduction

Waiting ✓ ✓

Non-utilzed talent ✓

Transportation ✓

Inventory

Figure 3.1

Once Hannah and Nathan have made their choices, Jay summarizes.

"Interesting, you are both very aligned and observant. It seems that Waiting is the winner followed by Non-utilized Talent, and finally Defect."

Jay remembers how Audrey related the work they do as driving through a city full of traffic lights. When the lights are green, we move in our vehicles easily and smoothly from point to point. That is value-added work, giving customers of supply chain partners what they want when they need it, and in the amount required. Sometimes we are approaching an intersection and must slow down due to yellow lights. That is non-value-added but necessary. We obey laws and regulations for safety and cooperation, we keep moving towards our destination but at a slower pace. At some point during a longer trip, we will have to stop at a red light. No movement, no progress towards our next destination. This is pure waste from the perspective of our customer who is waiting for us to arrive with our goods and services.

"I'll email you both a longer description of each of those words after lunch. Let's focus on our top three for now: Waiting, Non-utilized Talent, and Defects."

Jay returns to the whiteboard and writes out a few lines after each of the top three before Hannah and Nathan.

"Waiting is delayed action and also includes process step delays or work stoppages.

Non-utilized talent is the under-utilized abilities of people left unused/ ignored.

Defects waste human effort to inspect and fix errors."

Jay turns to Hannah and Nathan to ask them for examples.

They discuss examples of Waiting including wasted time doing nothing until instructions get shared, delays in informational meetings to occur, material shipments, waiting for people to make decisions, delays until the next production step begins, or even waiting time associated with recapping the meeting due to Nathan joining the meeting late.

For Non-utilized Talent, they discuss the waste associated with ignoring improvement ideas from junior team members often doing the value-added work. Jay shares how Audrey expands the definition to include policies or procedures that restrict employees' responsibilities from making routine decisions or improving.

For Defects, Hannah shares examples of overworked team members making mistakes in calculations, drawing details, and estimates. Nathan explains how even mistakes in spreadsheet cells contribute to non-compliant work resulting in wasted efforts to make corrections later or pass low-quality work to others.

"Let's break for lunch and catch up again this afternoon. I have a few others to catch up with before we get back into discussing Scrum," Jay suggests.

Jay's after-lunch email included the following DOWNTIME definitions and examples.

- Defects are the waste associated with the human effort involved in inspecting for and fixing errors. Mistakes in calculations, drawings, estimates, spreadsheet data entry errors, or non-compliant work are all examples.

- Overproduction is the waste associated with the unnecessary human effort producing work in excess or ahead of customer requirements. Think of designing details before they are needed by the next discipline, printing paperwork before it's needed, or installing more work than required by the next trade.

- Waiting: Waiting means delays or stoppages. Examples include waiting for instructions, delayed material shipments, waiting for people to make decisions, delays until the next production step begins, or even waiting time associated with running slow computers.

- Non-utilized Talent: The under-utilized abilities of people is the waste associated with ignoring improvement ideas from people closest to the value-producing work. It even includes policies or procedures that restrict employees' responsibilities from making routine decisions or improving.

- Transportation: Avoid unnecessary movement of things that don't change the value of the work. An example could be sequential process steps separated by distances requiring shipping due to not being co-located or moving files from one location to another. This includes shipping prefabricated materials from offsite production facilities or stick building onsite with materials shipped in from manufacturing.

- Inventory: Avoid holding onto information or materials longer than required. For example, piles of finished materials not yet needed, unprocessed work, unread emails, or overstocked marketing materials.

- Motion: Motion means non-value-added movements of people such as unnecessary meetings or walking to the copier and printer instead of utilizing paperless business processes.

- Excessive Processing: Unnecessary activities due to complex processes and systems such as too many approvals or an application form that requires the same data in different places.

Later that afternoon, the three get back together. Jay opens up the meeting with a question.

"What challenges do you imagine will prevent this office from piloting one Scrum team this month?" "Jay, I originally thought this would be extra work and effort to make this office more like San Francisco. After our whiteboard session this morning, I realize that I was engaged in a few things that were zapping my time and impeding my team's progress. If this can help Avi and his project, what's our next step?" Hannah shares her thoughts.

Nathan looks surprised but nods before adding:

"I will support our team. I'm not sure how this is going to look. I don't see any examples of this in Arizona. Some of our people are going to see this as another California-based initiative. There will be resistors."

Jay smiles and thanks them both for their honesty.

"Let's start with Avi and his team as a pilot. Having been a resistor before, I can relate to how some are going to feel about this change. We can learn and iterate with a few people to see what works here for our people and project teams. Hannah can evaluate who has some spare capacity to support Avi permanently. He will need some help to make some small shifts. We need to make some space so he can get at least half an hour freed up each day for the rest of this week and next.

The rest of the week has a few ups and downs. Avi is grateful to get some help and outwardly nervous that Jay is going to be meeting with him daily for the rest of the week. He repeatedly asks Hannah whether he is getting fired. She reassures him each time and starts sharing some of the concepts Jay taught her and Nathan. Hannah and Nathan agree to set up follow-up meetings with Audry and Avi. The short-term plan is to have Avi lead his team in a daily stand-up meeting this week and next. Jay and Audrey would be back in person in two weeks to see what is working and what to do next. Hannah gets curious and even makes it to most of Avi's daily meetings. She notices how much higher the engagement is compared to their typical project team status update calls.

Jay connects with Peter back in San Francisco and shares the progress being made. Peter asks him to write a short summary for the company newsletter showcasing the one company approach and spotlighting people experimenting with new ways of working.

"This pilot may not be successful, Peter," Jay raises his doubts.

"Don't worry, there are dozens of other project teams to pilot next," Peter replies. "Our goal is to enable the office to adopt Scrum across all projects."

Peter remains as persistent today as when Jay began working for him all those years ago.

Audrey and Avi develop good rapport and quickly move from doing only daily team stand-up meetings to closing other project meetings with short 5-minute plus/delta dialogue to solicit ideas to increase meeting effectiveness and work quality.

She shares the whole Scrum framework with Avi on a whiteboard over lunch. Avi realizes that they are already doing many parts of Scrum. Audrey smiles and they talk about building up towards the entire framework one week at a time.

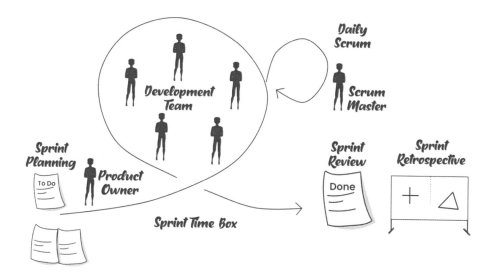

Figure 3.2

Avi is iterating into the whole framework with his project team as their capacity increases and as their needs change. Avi told Jay that before this pilot started, he was getting burned out and didn't even feel confident in taking some needed time off. Now he feels in more control of how the work is being done. He is also noticing the client's satisfaction rising. Jay is very pleased and anticipates what Peter is going to say at their next meeting: " Let's go and make a difference together."

A couple of months later, Peter and Jay visit the Phoenix office together. They are both greeted warmly by Nathan. Before going to see Avi and his team, Nathan asks them to come to his office first. There on the whiteboard wall, adjacent to his desk, is a small Scrum board.

Nathan explains how he bumped into Audrey in the kitchen one morning making coffee and they got to talking about workflow. They kept talking and carried on into his office where Audrey drew a small four-column board of "Backlog, To Do, Doing, and Done."

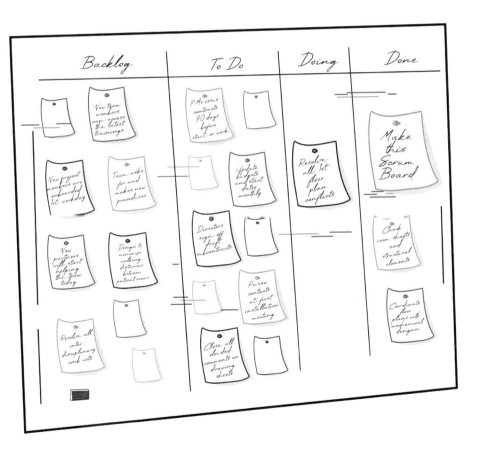

Image 3.1

Nathan points to his board.

"Look here on my backlog. I have more than a few stubborn items out of my tattered notepad. Thanks to using Scrum, I'm now able to see progress and priority on my responsibilities. It's the first time I'm seeing and moving the work in a prioritized way. I can see now how I wasn't working on what I thought was most important and urgent. I was also kidding myself that I was multitasking well. Audrey is amazing. Thank you, Jay, for giving us this opportunity, you are going to love our new way of working embracing Scrum."

Chapter 4

Think, Do, Be

Eric is obsessed with strategy and problem-solving. He spent the last few years working on large, highly collaborative projects for healthcare owners. As the onsite director, he kept a close eye on how the $700M project was going and where. A few years ago he read *"Good to Great"* by Jim Collins. This project could be great. So many large project teams are not great and a good many have high turnover and dissatisfied clients.

Eric remembers reading that something like 98% of mega-sized projects over $1 billion fail to meet their original objectives.

Reinventing Construction: A Route to Higher Productivity

Eric shifts back in his office chair reflecting on the progress of the project. The 70 person team generates a lot of emails. The team is new, all have experience but none have worked together before. If they get the shell buildout of level 3, this job will be over $1 billion.

It is 7 pm and the office is quiet. The last team members left an hour ago. He looks at the draft agenda for tomorrow's team meeting, just a blinking cursor in Word. Eric decides to Scrum the meeting in the morning and head home for the night.

Eric remembers that he has a podcast episode about how lean thinking, right actions, and better outcomes will make some good inspiration for the long drive home. In his car, he turns the radio on:

"Audience, please welcome our guest, Felipe Engineer-Manriquez. He knows how to lay a foundation of respect for people and ignite the mindset of continuous improvement in order to deliver construction projects on budget, on time, with great safety."

Eric thinks that this is perfect timing, his job is on budget, almost on time, and safe.

"Listen in as we dive into the mindset shift that people need to adopt in order to be able to collaborate together as a team to deliver the results that the owners of construction projects are looking for. Felipe has a unique way of looking at the construction business and delivering the information that you're going to find super helpful. So feel free to check out his podcast, The EBFC Show. I'll put the link in the show notes. Felipe, welcome to the Smart Builder podcast."

"Thank you, Michael. It's nice to be here, and I appreciate the opportunity to talk about some of my favorite subjects in the construction business.

"Felipe, why do you love to talk about the construction business so much?"

"Business in my mind, Michael, is fundamentally an exchange between people. In the building business, individuals and more often teams of people come together for win-win situations. Why not have fun, and get paid at the same time? Why not give people what they need, and have them benefit from it immediately."

"Alright Felipe, one of my clients is a project manager with a large engineering company. He is very successful but often says that construction is difficult because of the people. Sometimes projects even suck. What do you say to that?"

"Tell your friend that he's got room for improvement. Because yeah, it is challenging. I wouldn't say projects suck. I've had bad experiences in construction. Yes, that's a fact. I've had challenges. I've had days where I ask myself, why am I doing this? But on a whole? I absolutely love it. When I was a kid, I got a chance to get into technology early on. I often annoyed my parents by taking things apart. They thought it would be great to put that energy into engineering school instead of objects in their home. So that's what I went to school for. But I got bit by the construction bug. I toured a construction project onsite at school, and I fell in love with construction right away. You know Michael, why would I make something like a phone that people can throw away in less than two years when I can be part of making a building? Buildings are really hard to throw away."

"That's beautiful Felipe. We talked about strategy prior to hitting the record button. You mentioned strategic problem-solving. So in terms of running a construction project, what do you mean by strategic problems?

"Every single job has its challenges and requires strategic problem-solving. Everything that we build, whether it's a highway, a bridge, a solar field, a hospital, a new tenant improvement space, or just upgrading an office, involves solving a problem for the client, a building owner. Owners are involved in their business. Most generate revenue for goods/services and nonprofits provide services for a collective/group. We create this physical thing for them. And by changing their physical environment, they are now able to solve their problem. There's a strategy to that. Everything we build, some of the things are easier than others. Let's take the simple example of a school."

Eric shifts in his car seat and turns up the volume. This is exactly what I need for tomorrow. We definitely are solving a problem with this new hospital.

"If we're building a school, the strategic problem that a school is solving, whether it's a brand new campus or extending an existing one is creating an environment to get more students educated. The point of the school is to give students a place to learn and grow. If it's a hospital, it could be delivering better patient care. If we're building a new testing facility for a clinic, it might be about streamlining the process so that we can test more people during the pandemic. The pandemic is absolutely testing a lot of healthcare systems and providers out there. So, building clinic testing laboratories creates a solution for doctors and patients. That's strategic problem-solving. What we're then doing with the building process in design and construction is tactical. We're bringing strategy to life. That's what I really absolutely love, and I have a framework that is just darn near perfect, that allows people to have that strategic impact, much faster with less effort. And it's totally free."

"Felipe, that is excellent. Let me just back up a little bit. So, when you're using this idea of strategic problem solving, you're taking it from the perspective of the client. They have a problem that they want to solve, and therefore they are engaging people with construction services. In order for a company to be successful, they need to have the client's perspective on that problem prior to executing the tactics. Am I following that right?"

"That is exactly right. I'm saying if they want exceptional success, they need to understand the client's problem. Without that, you are going to have mediocre success or failure."

Eric pauses the podcast as he enters his driveway. This meeting for tomorrow was requested by the owner. He hadn't even considered why or asked them who else should be invited. Eric gets inside and resumes the podcast at the kitchen table while his food heats up in the microwave.

"Companies today, companies that you and I know as household names are making money by accident every day."

"Felipe, I was talking to this one company yesterday and I wish we'd recorded this show before then. I am just amazed at how people have these barriers in their minds to engaging deeper in their business."

"The hardest thing for most people, Michael, is just to start with a bit of lean thinking first. Step one is to understand the client's perspective. Let's break it down by a series of questions. If you're in construction and a general contractor, or trade partner, or a designer, an architect, or an engineer offering services, you're likely responding to a client's request for proposal. Inside of that request for proposal, there's going to be a lot of words, a lot of jargon, maybe even a picture or two, or maybe not. Or you could even just have a conversation with a building owner about their needs. A lot of the time in the design community, designers get involved in these conversations early on, because they're already doing something for the client, the client is describing this problem they're trying to overcome. Let's take a healthcare example to make this a bit more concrete for the listeners. A hospital might have extremely long waiting times and struggle to treat patients with care and efficiency due to the existing building layout and technology. They will say things along the lines of adding more patient beds to increase capacity. They're looking at the numbers, and they're looking at the way that they're treating patients today. The forecast is predicting that they're going to crash against their current capacity, which means they're going to one day turn people away, and people are not going to get care. So as an architect, as an engineer working on a project, or a general contractor we latch onto adding more patient beds. This may be solved by putting together a team to build a new addition. A request for proposal might be very prescriptive and say that the building is going to be new. It will be three stories tall and have 100 beds in it. How do we approach this with better actions?

The right action is to act like a builder and a business person. Seek to understand what problem the customer is trying to overcome. Ask questions like:

- What specific improvement in their current business operations are they trying to achieve?

- How does the building solve their problem?

- Who can we talk to about this?

- When can we walk through their current operations to understand their culture and workflows?

- What performance metrics will be measured after the building is constructed that the owner will use to determine the fit of the solution?

Asking these types of questions gets us into a strategic mindset, a lean mindset putting the customer's needs first. When a team works on this with the owner's input, you magically gain alignment."

Eric's microwave beeps again. Now his food is getting cold but his notepad is filling. He sketches out a mini Scrum board on the next blank page.

New Team Member Onboarding Planning Meeting		
To Do	**Doing**	**Done**
Introductions		
Answer as a team how this new hospital delivers on the owner's needs for patients.		
Explore what metrics are important during design, construction, and future operations.		

Table 4.1

Eric has been using Scrum boards during meetings on this project in place of printed meeting agendas. The team really liked the visual and tactile nature of whiteboard Scrum. This wouldn't be new for tomorrow but the questions and thinking would be.

"Next, you put those responses down on paper or on a whiteboard. It doesn't matter if it's digital or analog. Now all people are actually involved in responding. Together they are facing the customer's problem and collaborating on the right set of actions."

"This looks like a roadmap to success."

"You are on the path, Michael, but don't skip the journey. Just like that, we become part of the owner's team and now are ready to engage on the next step, closing the gap. Every subsequent action we do, making decisions included, either puts us closer to solving the owner's problem or further away. Strategy in the simplest form is setting direction. Now we've got to take action to get there and select the right tactics. Design and construction are all about making something from nothing, bringing ideas into reality. As a team, we can ask ourselves questions like these:

- What trade-offs do we need to make?

- Does this process help or hinder the customer from getting this building on time, on budget, with the desired quality?

- What can we measure or observe to judge progress towards the strategic goal?

Trade-offs for many building professionals often raise conflicts."

"Construction projects usually start with idealistic visions and schedules. Teams are only teams in name if individual needs are put ahead of the project's."

"Yes, that's typical. This process reduces adversarial conflict by putting the problem in front of people. Often these questions are put on A3 sheets of paper. In the United States, we put it on 11" by 17" sheets. This changes the dynamics of how we're engaging. If I bring up an issue and put it on our shared problem-solving place, we look at it together instead of shooting the messenger. It helps support project-first thinking. The focus goes back to the problem the customer is trying to solve with the project."

"Collaboration will increase when we stop seeing people as the problem. So the way I look at this is that we're defining a game that we're going to play. Like, if you want to play the game, then these are the rules of the game. Answering the questions helps you win."

"That's it, Michael, perfect analogy. The next thing to do in the strategic problem-solving game is to engage the project partners on the strategy. The people doing the work will give us the best insights into what is happening. We call that the current condition. I'm talking about these six people, or these two dozen people or these 100 people, however many people you have on your project. Socialize the questions a bit.

This can be used on any project even if it is well underway, you know, shovels in the ground, sooner, or even later. Knowing and understanding the current condition will help the team see the metrics and key performance indicators. It is just like a doctor asking you how you are doing, getting your response, and still taking your temperature. Budget and schedule are two obvious metrics to measure. But both are lagging indicators for project progress. Safety, however, is a leading indicator. If the job site is benefiting from good safety protocols, everything's doing really well. You won't see many first aid incidents or recordable injuries. If you're starting to have accidents, or you've had an injury, you're likely behind schedule. Right schedule progress and healthy budget spending are interrelated, they come as a pair."

"This sounds a bit different from how I grew up in construction, Felipe. Say I'm listening to this podcast and I'm a general contractor that typically does design, bid, build projects. I've made some money and survived adversarial project teams and stuff like that. How do I begin to make that mindset shift?"

"It is as I said at the beginning. You begin with strategy by thinking about answers on what is the purpose of this thing you're building. All your listeners have heard it and now their minds are on it. That's the first step, lean thinking. No general contractor that I know can do a turnkey building today. It's just too complicated and too complex. There are too many specialty trades needed, especially for hospitals. Project first thinking will become a habit with daily practice even if you're still doing design, bid, then build."

Eric eats his dinner and realizes the whole team has only had design, bid, build experience. This is their first collaborative project and his first design-build project.

"Felipe, in your experience, let's say we've defined the game we're going to play, we understand the problem that the client is looking to solve. We have a group of well-meaning trade partners, contractors, designers, clients, and the whole team is on the same page, and yet the project isn't delivered successfully. Why does that happen?"

"That's a great question, Michael. It likely comes down to design-making speed or decision latency. Two major things occur in parallel during a project, think of them as flows. There's a workflow that everyone can see, we can go out and engage with design and can walk through the building spaces as construction progresses. The people, machinery, materials, and methods are visible and flowing. And then there's this invisible flow moving in the opposite direction called an information flow. This invisible part is what stops most projects from being successful. I was just talking to my friend that earns a living as a forensic scheduler. Google that, it is a real job. They work as part of a legal team hired by construction firms to win lawsuits against building owners. Apparently, you can make a good living in construction lawsuits. They learn to look for the information flows to break down how projects fail. Following the information, flow helps to unveil clues and find when and what started going badly. My friend said an information flow clue will often show up in a daily report. These journal-like entries are written by foremen. In other cases, the clues show up in meeting minutes or requests for information items."

"Okay, let's talk about this information flow a little bit more. What can I do as a part of the team to ensure that that information flow is happening in such a way that we avoid project failure?"

"Michael, it depends on the team. If your team is co-located, which means that everyone's working together in the same office space, you can create a more open environment. Just because we're physically inside four walls doesn't mean that we're actually collaborating. Set some rules of engagement. Using the game analogy, set up the game rules so that everyone succeeds. Let people know that it's okay to not send an email, it's preferred to talk to somebody face-to-face. Do we have more people sending emails after five o'clock at night and carbon copying the world, or do we have more impromptu conversations? So, if I'm a project manager and I'm talking to a superintendent about an issue and right beside me stands a silent project engineer, I need to observe body language to see if the messages are being received. Meetings are another example worth noting."

Eric pushes his plate away and grabs his pen and pad of paper again. This podcast is getting all the things he needs for tomorrow's meeting.

" Some people, believe it or not, think that going to a lot of meetings makes them important. They also feel important being invited to meetings. As human beings, we need to belong in order to feel whole. If there's a meeting going on and I'm not invited, it will make me wonder why and what is being talked about without me. In the analogy of the game, set up the rules of engagement at the beginning, make it clear what meetings are occurring and who should be attending."

Eric opens his phone and double checks the meeting invitation. He didn't include an agenda and the "New Team Member Onboarding Planning" title left lots to the imagination. He taps play on his phone.

"Let's outline and be clear on what we want. If you're working with a team, Michael and they are in a lot of meetings, there's an unwritten policy that says being in meetings is good, and that unwritten policy is crushing people's productivity. Many meetings are not run very well. If you're sitting in a meeting and the whole thing goes by without you making a contribution, why were you there? Many projects have an unwritten policy that the leaders need to be at every meeting to know what's going on and guide it. I found that is an unproductive anti-lean way of thinking. Develop the people a little bit more, trust that you hired talented people capable of doing the right things, and touch base periodically as needed. Make your meetings more visual. Put in a process to support visual management, visual cues, to make problems visible, so that people can solve them."

Eric flips back to his Scrum board thinking that he could have taken a picture of this and emailed it as the agenda for the meeting. In the same email, he could have asked for feedback and instructed people to forward the meeting to those they thought should attend. It seemed so obvious now.

"Michael, don't worry if you have never done this yet. It's a good thing to have problems, they inform us where to spend our energy. Make them visible and solve them. This is a different approach. Some teams would rather quickly deal with an issue and sweep it under the rug as fast as possible. On those projects, problems are not good, and they're not welcomed. You know that you are in one of those projects when someone says to you, as you're explaining a challenging situation, don't bring me problems, bring me solutions. That's a sign that problems are not okay. Visual projects that celebrate problems do exist, though. I went to a large healthcare project and they posted their budget on the whiteboard in the main conference room for everybody to see."

"Felipe, can construction companies make money on conflict projects with low transparency?"

"Yes, some make a great living on that high-conflict, high-adversarial approach. At some point, people get frustrated, realize that they won't live forever, and get tired of the fighting. Why not have a little bit of fun while you're out there?"

"So strategic problem solving, Felipe. We started off by identifying the problem that the client is looking to solve. We've talked about putting this in action with our team using questions. What do we do next?"

"Next, we assess the current state of how this team is working together. This approach will bring forward key performance indicators that are important to your organization and your team. Remember what we said about safety as a leading indicator, team morale is another leading indicator for project success. Let's do something. Let's take action and assess where you are now compared to what the owner wants. We take action to close that gap. Start an experiment. If communication on your team is not flowing smoothly, maybe people are tied up in meetings all day, and the throughput on work is low. Consider eliminating some non-productive meetings. That's an action step that you can take this week. There isn't a perfect solution for any problem, so try a few experiments and see what works for your team. Use your intuition to guide you, but come up with a series of countermeasures. These can be short, long-term, or a mix of both. Finally, make adjustments based on what the team learns and keep going through the process until the gaps are closed."

"Thank you, Felipe, this has been a mindset shifter. What advice do you have for people new to this way of thinking?"

"Michael, thank you, it has been a pleasure. My number one advice would be to be curious. That's going to get you into more strategic problem-solving. That's the most important thing. The second thing, phone a friend for help when needed. There is a lot of information out there, talk to somebody that's got some experience so that they can assess where you are right now. You can contact me as well. Michael has graciously added my contact information to the show notes. Talking with somebody with experience will get you better outcomes because they can recognize where you are and help you get where you want to go quickly. The final thing, do an experiment. All this information without any kind of action is waste."

"Felipe, I really, really appreciate your time. This was a lot of fun. I got a lot out of this conversation."

"Thank you, Michael."

Eric looks back over this scribbled Scrum board. Felipe is right. In Scrum, the team does the value-added work that serves the building's purpose. He adds their goal.

New Team Member Onboarding Planning Meeting

To Do	Doing	Done	Goal: Build a healthy place in Anytown, USA, that advances cures, prevention, and overcomes diseases through caring patient treatment.
Introductions			
How does this new hospital deliver patient care?			
What metrics are important during construction and operations?			
What do we need for new project team members to experience on day one?			

Table 4.2

Eric arrives at work the next morning. He is the first one in. By the time the team shows up a few minutes later, the conference room whiteboard is already a match to his evening's Scrum board notes. The team starts coming in and one by one they read the board's tags and goal. Some look at him with smiles and a few are skeptical and sitting cross-armed. In less than thirty minutes Eric gets confirmation that the tags in the To

Do list are correct and in priority order with a bonus improvement on the goal with a small value-adding change.

Build a healthy place in Anytown, USA, that advances cures, prevention, and overcomes diseases through caring patient treatment where everyone remains friends after the project is complete.

In the next 30 minutes, the team discusses each topic. The smiling people are still smiling. The crossed armed people give their opinions on each tag and Eric gives them new tags to expand, change, and provide responses. Everyone shares and every share gets a tag making the Scrum board the hub of the meeting. The conference room table gets pushed back at some point and the meeting continues with all standing at the board. Eric makes a mental note to send Felipe a review thanking him for sharing how to use Scrum in more ways on his project. As the meeting closes, each agrees that this process works and unanimously recommends using Scrum for new team member onboarding.

2
PART

THE BENEFITS
OF SCRUM
PATTERNS

Chapter 5

The Benefits of Scrum Patterns

Let's play. Start with knowing the rules of the game. I want you to have fun and win daily. Just like scaffolding is used as a framework in design and construction to give us access to progress with a building, so does the Scrum framework enable valuable work to flow. The Scrum framework does not have all possible problem solutions. However, Scrum patterns help elicit a likely solution when problems arise (I guarantee they will). . You will find over 200 Scrum patterns in the Scrum Book *The Spirit of the Game.*

Let's start with the why first.

I've come to think of work as a game, especially project work, and I share this idea with many others. In 1993, a group of Scrum Pattern Language professionals (originally known as The Hillside Group) gathered in Colorado. They were inspired by the 1960s and 1970s work of a building architect, Christopher Alexander, on the theory of design and construction. Their work resulted in the publication of several books and a website that supports their experienced contributions to Scrum patterns, the Scrum PLoP Conference, and an open-source wiki. In 2011, they published a mission statement that resonates with my view of work as a game.

The Scrum PLoP Mission

Alistair Cockburn describes software development as a cooperative game. Scrum provides one set of rules for one such way of playing the game. The Scrum Guide is the official rulebook. However, the Scrum Guide doesn't tell you the rationale behind Scrum as a whole, or behind many of its successful practices. Those rationales come out of experience, community, and the insights of its founders and inventors. The Scrum PLoP mission is to build a body of pattern literature around those communities, describing those insights, so we can easily share them with the Scrum and Agile communities.

History of the Patterns

Let's honor our work and play with the *"Spirit of The Game"* in our minds and hearts. We are introducing something new, therefore, it's important to establish a supportive culture focusing on:

- Leading by example

- Adopting the five Scrum Values

- Following the spirit of the Agile Manifesto

Here are some examples from the design and construction industry.

- A project manager, superintendent, or lead designer approaches a team member with the demand to stop working on the current task to shift to another without any further explanation.

- An executive demands a milestone delivery date for a given increment of work.

- A project manager is uncomfortable with the team's self-organization and actively micro-manages them.

- A manager says something to the effect of "in the spirit of continuous improvement" before pressuring the Scrum team to a specific Scrum tracking tool (software, metrics, etc).

These examples don't technically contradict the Scrum Guide nor the spirit of the Agile Manifesto. As a current or future Scrum practitioner reading this book, you will, however, understand how these examples violate Scrum, negatively impact productivity, and make work much less fun.

Let's embody a culture that builds people up, builds projects that dazzle owners, and keeps everyone engaged in the process. To lead by example you need capacity and a good reason why which can be framed as a goal. Two great patterns to increase capacity and formulate a goal are:

- Good Housekeeping, Pattern 80

- The Sprint Goal, Pattern 71

Regardless if you are new to Scrum or have been using it since the 90s, these patterns will help you and your teams right now. I use them both most often with new and mixed experience teams to set a fertile environment of growing support and mutual trust.

Good Housekeeping: Pattern 80

In Lean Construction circles, it is more and more accepted that a clean site tends to be safer, on time, and more likely to be aligned with financial goals. Clean projects are also happier places to build, we all know of many examples of dirty projects that are far from happy. Some formal housekeeping programs have become popular in multiple industries including construction since Henry Ford instituted CANDO in his Model T assembly factories. It was later learned by Japanese automobile manufacturers and instituted in Japan as 5S and again made popular in the United States. Both acronyms have the same intention and are defined as follows:

CANDO	5S – English	5S – Japanese	Action Questions
Cleanup	Sort	Seiri	Are these things necessary, and, if so, how much is needed right here, right now?
Arrange	Set in Order	Seitori	Where is a better place to locate these things, and how much of them should be here to be useful?
Neatness	Shine	Seiso	What cleaning methods are needed where, by whom, when, and how to keep the work neat?
Discipline	Standardize	Shitsuke	What standard do we need to maintain the needed conditions in response to the answers above and who will daily help us to avoid setbacks?
Ongoing inprovement	Sustain	Seiketsu	What resources do we need to seek perfection, such as recognition for good housekeeping and resources, to support the implementation by leaders and team members, while keeping the creativity of all workers engaged, heard, and ideas implemented?

Table 5.1

Your team needs to make progress towards delivering value in the most frictionless way to allow for a smooth workflow. The current Sprint goal requires a clean starting point. If you or your team are spending energy on deciding what and where to start with, you have an opportunity to implement good housekeeping. Start where you find the biggest mess. People will immediately appreciate it and see the cleaned environment as a win. Remember that we all live in glass houses, so don't go rushing to point out another team member's mess before you clean your own working space first.

Bad housekeeping is visible and leads to poor team morale. If your office entrance has overflowing trash bins or furniture blocking the path to the seating areas, desks, or restrooms, you have multiple opportunities to improve the first impression for your staff and visitors. Messy or dirty conference rooms and restrooms simply aren't ready for meetings, coordination, problem-solving, or collaboration. If your team has to clean up these areas before they can start working, people are wasting valuable time.

The same applies to construction sites. If someone leaves a mess installing their work, the subsequent value creator can't begin until this mess is cleared. Messy work also masks the real state of design completion or installed work quality. If the team is unaware of the true work state or progress, there is a high likelihood of duplication of efforts and repeating work, which again is a waste of time and energy. If we aren't clean with our work, team members will have to invest energy to determine what has already been done before they can focus on the next task. Think back upon last week, how much time did you spend sifting through mountains of emails, meeting minutes, requests for information, plan change sketches, or even on outdated information radiators. It remains a challenge to separate the right information (signal) from the unneeded information (noise). Value as defined by your customer or supply chain partner is the beneficial transformation of information, materials, or a combination of both. If we prioritize and value our time, let's do the same for those we work with.

The time taken to clean adds no value for our customers. However, not allowing yourself or the team to clean up the workspace at all, will waste even more time and slow down the workflow. As you and the team make progress on a particular part of the design and construction work, much of the value-adding efforts may be near the end of the Sprint. Bad housekeeping will sharply decrease the ability to make progress. For Scrum teams using velocity, the team's number of points per Sprint will decrease. Velocity is a Scrum measure of the amount of work a Scrum Team can accomplish during a single Sprint. Velocity is calculated at the end of the Sprint by totaling the Points for all fully completed Sprint Backlog Items. Bad housekeeping may also lower the quality of work being handed off to subsequent supply chain partners receiving the team's work. The work environment that is messy hinders the team's progress and prevents team members and stakeholders from seeing the actual situation. Equally, workplaces and general working areas obscure or hide the actual state of progress, current situation, and visibility for handoffs. Undisciplined teams continuously spend time working in nonideal environments that hinder their work and rob them of their sense of accomplishment and pride.

It is critical to maintaining a completely clean environment for the workers and the work. Cleaning as you go requires far less effort than big batch cleanup efforts. Cleaning up at the end of the day, shift, period, or installation scope will allow for higher transparency for all team members on what work is ready, needed and by when. A clean environment allows for tasks to flow more smoothly. Disciplined teams continuously focus on maintaining clean work states. When anyone on the team can safely start working on the right thing at the right time you are in a continuously useful environment with flowing work and flowing information. Continuously keeping the ongoing work areas in shape raises confidence about the quality to all who see the work, especially your customers. Since people can see the true progress of the work, it is easier for the team to pull in work tasks for the current increment which makes even more progress towards the Sprint goal. The work must be in the 'Done' state as often as possible, ideally every day. Done means that the team has progressed the work sufficiently to their definition and the next phase of design or construction can begin.

The team is creating regular work increments in design or construction and the transient state is visibly making progress towards attaining the Sprint goal. Standards are not words, catchy phrases, policies, or input for posters but set by the team for good housekeeping.

Instituting a clean desk policy could mean that it's time to declutter and let go of old notes, sketches, or files. Use common sense and respect the team's culture to maintain a continuous focus on the balance between too little and too excessive Good Housekeeping. Freely borrowing from the ideas and successful implementation by others across other industries. Some learned about 5S being used within the Toyota Production System as noted in The Toyota Way Fieldbook: A practical guide for implementing Toyota's 4P's (sort, set in order, shine, standardize, and sustain) for good housekeeping. Alternatively, some prefer using Henry Ford's CANDO acronym that stands for clean up, arrange, neatness, discipline, and ongoing improvement. This pattern is about developing disciplined work habits which, among other things, results in a clean work area.

Good Housekeeping may often involve you and your team to clean up messes made by others. Robert Stevenson Smith Baden-Powell, the father of the Boy Scouts often said, "Try and leave this world a little better than you found it." That idea lives on with the Scouts that now have made it one of their slogans to say, "Leave the campground cleaner than when you found it."

Lord Baden-Powell Biography

The same slogan can be adapted to your team such as:

- 🏠 Leave the project trailer cleaner than when we entered it.

- 🏠 Leave the office cleaner than when we arrived.

- 🏠 Leave the job site cleaner than when we walked in.

- 🏠 Leave the studio cleaner than when we started drawing in it.

Good housekeeping requires intention and action. Good Housekeeping side effects will include increased commitment and stronger discipline from the entire team to maintain the clean workspace. The 5S methodology has been widely spread and there are numerous implementation examples about it worldwide. Although it is conceptually simple and does not require complex training or experts with sophisticated knowledge, it is essential to implement it through a rigorous and disciplined fashion **with** your team, not to your team.

Be aware that your team may be resistant at first and the time for cleaning will diminish the available time for critical work. This is an okay and normal response that may just be a sign that some processes and working tools need revision. Reasons for "why not" can now be addressed by the team as impediments. If they can't leave the work product in a clean state every day, this may indicate the problem is with the work itself. Let the team be a part of identifying the impediments to good housekeeping and iteratively work to remove the obstacles daily. The rules that the team collaboratively makes for maintaining good housekeeping should become part of the norms of conduct or team culture. Be mindful when new team members join and include sharing the team's good housekeeping expectations and standards as part of their onboarding.

Good housekeeping contributes to the minimization of eight forms of waste (overproduction, inventory, transportation, motion, waiting, defects, over-processing, and non-utilized creativity). In Chapter Five: Special Scrum Considerations, I elaborate on how to recognize and remove each type of waste. Collaborative implementation of the Good Housekeeping Pattern increases people's involvement, teamwork, morale, health, and safety. As a result, your project team will benefit from also having reduced costs, variability, and uncertainty.

Sprint Goal Pattern

71

You are ready to embark on your first Scrum Sprint or you are a seasoned Scrum team member and are working with your team in the Sprint Planning meeting. The objective of a Sprint is to deliver value to the customer or receiving supply chain partner. The Sprint is one of the five Scrum events. It is short by design, of regular cycle duration, and typically a single work week but no longer than four weeks total. This regular timebox allows for a short iteration or works with enough time to deliver a meaningful increment of work that keeps the team focused. If you read the Scrum Guide, you will recall that all other Scrum Events take place during a Sprint.

What is a Sprint Goal? The Sprint Goal is the singular objective for the Sprint which is the team's commitment to what work will be done by the end of this sprint increment. The goal provides clarity so each team member understands exactly what is needed, who needs it, why it is needed, and how achieving it provides value. The Sprint Goal fosters positive alignment and helps create focus which encourages the whole Scrum Team to collaborate to produce value rather than work on individual efforts to other ends.

Without the Sprint Goal teams may default into following a list of sprint backlog ("To Do" list) items or tasks that don't necessarily result in the creation of the greatest value possible. Since the team lays out its work plan in terms of individual tasks or deliverables, it is rather easy to be trapped into picking an individual item and then working on it in isolation during the sprint. That dilutes the innovation potential that comes from the interactions between individual team members who bring different perspectives to the work. I've even seen office walls and cubicle dividers become physical barriers to continuous communication. When the team connects in the same space or shared environment, insights emerge in casual conversations and observations of what others work on along with how it is accomplished. Isolated team members will miss such opportunities to the detriment of the whole team.

Using the Sprint Goal Pattern when Sprint planning answers the 'Why' question for what we include and exclude for this Sprint. From experience, I know that once a team starts working on something, things often change and may even need replanning in-progress work to deliver value to the project stakeholders. Team members may miss days for planned vacations, sickness, or even experience variation in the needed materials, equipment, and access to skilled experts such as experienced tradespeople and designers.

As the sprint continues, new work may emerge from the team's latest insights and time for this will be included in the plan for experienced teams. New teams may not have enough experience in collaborating this way and may fail to plan for it. If changes occur, decisions will be made to either just follow the original work plan or deviate and miss delivering greater value.

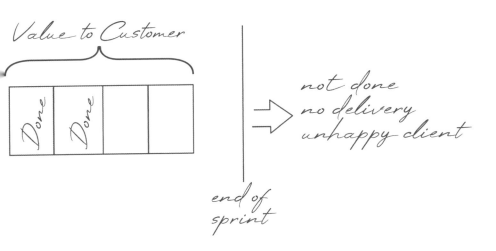

Figure 5.1

Another common issue is that partway through the sprint, the work situation changes enough that the team needs to replan. This could occur if it becomes clear that the team will not complete every single sprint backlog item (To Do List Tasks). Issues that can cause this to occur are job site accidents that require all team members to stand down, customer change directives, design changes to in-progress work, failed inspections, or abrupt changes to the team such as reassignment to another project. Some of these changes can cause the sprint backlog item work to expand in effort and time. The team still must deliver value and will need a goal to enable durable decisions for replanning the work for the remainder of the sprint

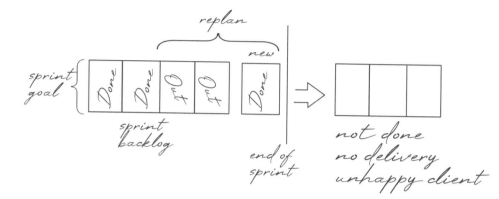

Figure 5.2

Another very common scenario is that the team needs critical technical knowledge about how to implement a particular part of the work. We may be building a mockup to validate a proposed architectural design for weather performance on an exterior wall assembly and need a special consultant to review the details or installation plan. The design team may need performance characteristics for new technology, such as new medical equipment, that can only be provided by a technical manufacturing representative. A well-developed product backlog item should identify such work, its uncertain requirements, and flag the team to get the right attention to focus on obtaining the knowledge rather than completing all the other planned work. The greatest value for this sprint might not be explicit from the current progress of the team's work product. The Sprint Goal can help the team frame the selection and appropriate detail of product backlog items for the Sprint and in this sense is more important than even the sum of the individually selected product backlog items.

Who on the team is best suited to make this type of goal in Scrum? The Product Owner will naturally guide the creation of the sprint goal because he or she has the best view on the next step toward the vision and how to create the greatest value. It is better to practice engaging the whole Scrum team in wording it to increase team-wide commitment to the goal. Many experienced product owners are adept at creating a compelling project vision that is executable by the team. Since they are ultimately responsible to curate and prioritize the Product Backlog, they can communicate the vision in a SMART goal for any given sprint.

SMART is an acronym attributed to Peter Drucker's Management by Objectives concept in the November 1981 issue of Management Review by George T. Doran. A search of the current meaning today typically returns common results including a statement that the goal is clear and reachable such that it passes these five criteria:

- Specific (simple and significant)
- Measurable (qualitatively or quantitatively meaningful to motivate action)
- Achievable (attainable)
- Relevant (reasonable and realistic)
- Time-bound (time-limited and time-sensitive).

An operations Scrum team may create a backlog item that states, "increase revenue by early progress billing by 5% this month." The team may devote so much effort to this single item that they sacrifice field coordination for an upcoming work phase that later decreases monthly billing due to delayed trade partners starting as planned. On the other hand, the majority of a sprint's value could be from a single critical product backlog item such as "passing fire alarm testing on the first attempt for a final certificate of occupancy." The scrum team commits to a short statement of the value it intends to create during the sprint. This single statement becomes the focus of all the work in the sprint. The 2020 Scrum Guide states that "The Product Owner proposes how the product could increase its value and utility in the current Sprint. The whole Scrum Team then collaborates to define a Sprint Goal that communicates why the Sprint is valuable to stakeholders. The Sprint Goal must be finalized prior to the end of Sprint Planning."

Well-crafted Sprint Goals can definitely be tied to project milestones or contract incentives that the team has agreed on to enhance project delivery. Achieving the goal should deliver value to the customer. Sprint goals help Scrum teams create a frame of what to include in this sprint as well as what to exclude. If you have been using Scrum and struggling with the team to select appropriate product backlog items for the sprint, I suspect you were lacking a Sprint goal or one that tied back to customer value. The goal creates coherence in the items you work on during the sprint and supports valuable work increments.

One example of a good initial approach is to express the Sprint Goal in the Product Backlog list. The product owner and the team can together elaborate and prioritize product backlog items under a given sprint goal. Here is an example from my backlog for this part of the book.

Since the proofreaders, editor, and I are all members of this autonomous Scrum book team, we must be able to manage ourselves to accomplish the goals, order the work plan, and be free to order Sprint Backlog how and wherever we see fit. The sprint goal is the sole mechanism by which the product owner can influence the potential order in which the team carries out its work by inferring urgency from the importance conveyed by the sprint goal. The team uses the goal to focus and commit to what work will be included in the sprint during sprint planning. Here is what the backlog became during sprint planning for this section of the book.

The team determined that "Create illustrations to support examples" was needed in order to achieve the goal while completing the other planned Sprint Backlog items. This is exactly the purpose of the sprint goal, to give the team a mechanism to define the details on how to accomplish the sprint goal by creating a sprint backlog. The column of cards closest to doing get

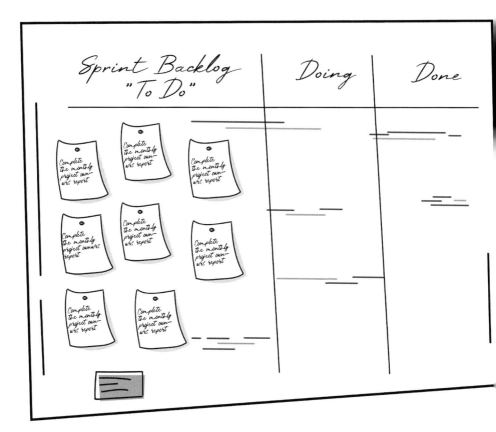

Figure 5.3

done first from top to bottom before the cards in column two and finally column three with just one item: Sprint Planning.

If the team concludes that they cannot accomplish the goal, they should refine the goal with the product owner. A key output of sprint planning is that the team should be able to explain how it can accomplish the goal and how it has achieved the goal at the end of the sprint. The ability to explain comes through understanding the work. This simple yet powerful explanation checkpoint is part of the sprint planning meeting and raises the probability that the team can actually achieve the goal within the sprint. The team commits to the sprint goal, which helps unify them on a common purpose and common work which aids in building trust. The sprint goal should be visible to the team as in the example above on the scrum board or some other information radiator. The team keeps the sprint backlog current during the sprint to support meeting the goal. The frequency of updates varies from team to team but it is part of their working agreement to show progress on the sprint backlog by moving the sticky notes to "Done" at the end of the day or in real-time as the work item progresses across the Scrum board to "Done."

Sometimes, it is possible to complete the goal before the end of the sprint without completing all the sprint backlog items. This actually helps the team respond to change and gives them the flexibility to adapt the plan during the Daily Scrum. As an example, emergent impediments, constraints, or bottlenecks can threaten the team's progress. When that happens, the team can automatically resort to the sprint goal as a plan B without expending long hours replanning. There is growing evidence that teams that expect changes more rapidly adapt and pivot to new plans without external coaching. The Sprint Goal helps teams make visible that the work being done is being done right and at the right time. Understanding the "why" of what the team does, helps enable rapid change when the team encounters something unexpected.

Jeff Sutherland goes on to elaborate how a Sprint Goal is critical to get everyone working together:

"In Silicon Valley in 2007, Palm was working on a Web OS [operating system] that was later acquired by Hewlett-Packard. Sprint to sprint the teams were doing well until they appeared to hit a wall in a couple

of Sprints. PBIs [product backlog items] were not getting finished. Developers were demotivated and going home early. I was brought in and got the Product Owners and Scrum Masters to spend an hour interviewing team members on why they demotivated. We found that they did not understand the reason why they were working hard on low-level PBIs. We spent an afternoon cleaning up the Product Backlog showing a clear linkage between high-level stories and a decomposition hierarchy. As soon as developers understood that the Sprint Goal was to improve performance of the Web OS by 10%, they were motivated to complete the low-level stories and velocity went back up to normal. Understanding why the PBIs are being implemented is critical for developers, particularly for expert developers who would prefer to go surfing if they don't see the reason for their work."

Better Sprint Goals usually relate to value delivery. The team can also define sprint goals in terms of process goals.

One example could be: "All new project engineers pair with the superintendent when writing questions for the design team to answer, typically called RFIs (requests for information)."

Another example: "All management team members attend the daily safety huddle each morning at 7 AM."

When you use a Sprint Goal supported by the entire team, each sprint gives the team greater opportunities for work buy-in and motivation for higher levels of engagement. Once a Sprint is finished, the next begins and you'll need to repeat this pattern to set another goal.

Chapter 6

I'm Not Satisfied With My Current Capacity

> *"Having no problems is the biggest problem of all."*
>
> **Taiichi Ohno**

If we can't understand our own capacity, we won't create awareness to change our habits. I often use a proxy to understand the throughput of a process, team, or system. The key questions below are intended to give you such a proxy. I intend to incite a personal intervention to interrupt your current work habits. I've put my pre-Scrum responses below. I encourage you to answer and reflect on these questions to find out how you can benefit from adopting Scrum:

Key Questions:

- What is my problem, struggle, or frustration with work now?

    I'm working more than six days per week and the pace of work isn't going to slow down anytime soon. I can't sustain this workload. I'm not healthy, I'm not happy, and I'm not present with my family when I'm at home.

- What is my current productivity level?

    I have no idea how productive I am. I'm in meetings most of the day and processing a mountain of paperwork at night. My performance review comments were vague but the message is clear: Work harder and you'll catch up soon.

- Am I able to do what is needed to help deliver my project(s)?

    No. I need to plan and see further ahead to enable the builders to put quality work in place. Right now I'm just firefighting today's problems.

🔲 How will I know whether or not I'm improving?

I don't know it because I'm just firefighting today's issues, I'm not improving my work, I'm just accomplishing it.

Until I learned about Scrum, these questions didn't even cross my mind. After discovering Scrum's evolution and applications, I started questioning what I was doing, and the framework helped me see the answers. My problem was simple, but I was lacking the awareness to initiate change.

Temporary night shifts had become my new normal. The long night drives with little distractions lent to improved reflections about my work and how I was contributing to our construction project's progress. I realized that working at night I was able to achieve all my office duties before our first break during the shift. I was wondering why I couldn't do the same during normal daytime work hours. Feelings of frustration and disappointment were my constant companions.

My team kept telling me that I should be "enjoying it" and that I'd be back on days soon. What was my problem? I guess it was the realization that I couldn't achieve that same level of productivity during the regular daytime workweek.

My output on day shifts was consistent but flat. As a general contractor, I was working as a trade manager on a hard bid, lowest qualified price contract for a private higher education client. The norm was that we would work at least 60 hours per week or you'd be labeled lazy regardless of your contributions. Excluding weekends (I worked several each month), I was still logging well over 60 hours per week and peaking above 70.

At the time, I was using Lean for five years already and would categorize everything I did in:

- Work that adds value.

- Work that doesn't add value but is necessary.

- Work that doesn't add value and is pure waste.

I managed to shift most of my output into category one. After working these night shifts, the sun literally set on that faulty feeling. I now recognized that I hadn't successfully mastered my own productivity. What was my current productivity? I didn't know the answer, so I set out to measure it.

At this point in my career, I was decently experienced with over a decade of construction experience ranging from wastewater treatment plants, schools, higher education, hospitals, tenant improvements, and working around the management office from preconstruction/ estimating through onsite operations including field supervision and project management. I had also been applying principles from Lean Manufacturing and did improve my output and effectiveness twofold getting all of my work done while no longer working over 100 plus hours per week. It wasn't that this work or project was radically different or new. The methods to manage large complex work involving dozens of firms and stakeholders carried with it a very familiar momentum of meetings, reports, change orders, and arguments about who the customer was and what the customer wanted. It was some kind of inertia that made me fall back into old habits learned and reinforced daily. My experiences kept repeating themselves, I didn't learn or grow, and that wasn't good enough.

My work hours started slipping back up and I was starting to do work from home. Most weekends included several hours catching up on email or compiling reports for the coming week. My health at that time did not compete well with the daily grind and family obligations often got sacrificed. By all measures of physical health, I was hitting rock bottom. I had gained over 20 pounds and my blood test results from my annual physical pushed my vitality age up by five years over my real age.

My annual performance reviews at work were identical to the previous saying something like this, "You are very dedicated and one of our hardest workers, keep it up and you'll be promoted soon." This was about the fourth or fifth time I'd heard that. My career was stalling, my health was failing, and my family wasn't happy with all the work I was putting in without any reward. Working more wasn't the solution. And I couldn't figure out how to change my situation.

Working the night shifts interrupted my typical habits. They created a small space to allow me some overdue reflection. I now had, by pure chance, a new perspective on my work. While driving home night after night for three weeks straight, I contrasted my previous day shift work versus my night shift work. Of many differences, one big one was the increased autonomy or ability to guide my priorities each shift so that handoffs to the day staff would be valuable and productive. Another strikingly large difference was the massive gain in productivity despite working fewer hours. I could see a definitive contrast between the night shift work and day shift work. Another big change was the increased planning and improved conversations I was having with our management team at the end of their day in preparation for the start of the night's work. This late afternoon debrief allowed for a summary of the day's key meetings and changing site conditions so our crews would be ready for the night's work schedule with the priority goal in mind. Previously, we were having a single staff meeting during the week on Monday afternoons in addition to other ad hoc and regularly scheduled owner and subcontractor meetings. Now, I was having multiple mini-meetings with our team informally but each following a similar agenda consisting of few priorities from each. These simple changes in information flow due to the circumstances dramatically improved my output and team communication. Now, I answered the question, "Am I able to do what is needed to help deliver my project?" More effective communication and planning changed my output and I started establishing new habits that worked regardless of assigned work schedule, day or night.

During this same time I was still listening to audiobooks driving to and from the project – a habit I had reinforced by years of construction project commuting. After a string of books about Lean, Audible recommended *Scrum: The art of doing twice the work in half the time* by Scrum co-creator Jeff Sutherland. The red book cover and title resonated so much with me that I downloaded it immediately. I devoured the book in three days.

Then, I started sprinting and experimenting with what I had learned.

Start Your First Sprint and Keep it Simple!

I highly recommend reading the 14-page Scrum Guide before you create your first Scrum Board. You need some sticky notes and a marker. Label your sticky notes with "To Do", "Doing", and "Done" and place them in a horizontal column on a wall (or whiteboard). You can add a

'Backlog' and other columns to organize your workflow, but I recommend keeping it simple in the beginning. The entire Scrum method consists of 11 main steps:

1. Pick a Product

2. Pick a Team

3. Pick a Scrum Master

4. Prioritize Backlog Items

5. Estimate the Backlog

6. Sprint Planning

7. Make your work visible

8. Daily Stand-up Meeting

9. Sprint Review

10. Sprint Retrospective

11. Repeat

Now you're ready to begin using Scrum in construction. Below is an example of how I applied the following 11 steps and delivered 20 negotiated change orders in 10 workdays that were billable that same month while still doing all my other daily work, job walks, and being off-site for meetings a day or two per week. That was on traditional design-bid-build project delivery. Today, I use the same steps with new individuals and teams.

1. **Pick a Product**

My pilot Scrum implementation involved change orders on a hard-bid project as the product. For a change order to be considered "Done" meant it was negotiated, accepted by the owner, and billable. You can add more project management workflows through the Scrum framework each subsequent Sprint. This pilot example focused only on change orders.

2. **Pick a Team**

The teams needed to have the competency to complete all the work in their backlog. Since this pilot focused on change orders, our team consisted of one owner's representative, numerous subcontractor project managers, trade managers, and one project accountant.

3. **Pick a Scrum Master**

I was our Scrum Master since I had done the above-mentioned preparation on Scrum.

4. **Create and Prioritize Backlog Items**

We allocated each change order to a sticky note and placed it in our "To Do" column on the Scrum Board. I ordered this list by placing the oldest to largest change orders on top followed by newer and smaller-sized change orders.

5. **Refine / Estimate the Backlog**

I then reordered the change orders in the list by prioritizing what the customer wanted first. Some changes required additional stakeholder review based on daily feedback from the owner's team.

6. **Sprint Planning**

    We spent 30 minutes organizing what was planned and communicating it to the team. Our goal was to get one change order done per day (but we quickly increased it to two to three per day ending with an average of two per day). More upfront planning made execution easier, so don't skip this step.

7. **Make Work Visible**

    We used a whiteboard and sticky notes on our construction office wall for all team members to see the post-it notes move along from one column to the other in order of "To Do", "Doing", and "Done". This visualization allowed the team and stakeholders to instantly know where we stood by simply looking at the board.

8. **Daily Stand-Up**

    Once each day, the team came together for 15 minutes to 'walk the board'. Each team member would answer just three questions.

    1. What did I do yesterday to finish the Sprint?

    2. What will I do today to finish the Sprint?

    3. Are there obstacles blocking the Sprint Goal?

    The answer to question three became a task and was finished next before moving onto other work. Our single, cross-functional team had the functional skills and responsibilities to resolve impediments. As the Scrum Master, I owned impediment removal and had to make problems visible to the right team member for resolution. People's money for completed work was a really good motivator to make impediment removal a high priority at all times.

9. **Sprint Review**

    We held a short team meeting at the end of each Sprint to evaluate what was accomplished and then refine the remaining backlog or tasks incorporating feedback from the team.

10. **Sprint Retrospective**

    We asked these four questions to focus the team on the goal and encourage learning:

    What went well?

    What can be improved?

    What can we do right now to achieve a better outcome?

    What is our velocity?

    Our two-week average velocity measured in change orders was ten per week. The building trades really liked the speed of change order reviews and approvals. One example of a better suggestion was to preview change order entitlement with the owner's representative before making a change order tracking number with the potentially impacted building trade project managers. We made that improvement by using a collaborative email exchange that resulted in the owner agreeing or disagreeing with the scope change. This step saved countless hours of unnecessary data entry and debating among project team members.

11. **Repeat**

    Completing a single Sprint enabled work to flow. Repeat the

cycle consistently for exponential value delivery with less effort.

Spend any amount of time in conversation with me and it is impossible not to notice how excited I get about Lean Construction and Agile frameworks, especially Scrum. It all started with a small experiment. Launch your pilot now. Don't worry about finding the perfect project or perfect time. As Dr. Jeff Sutherland says, "Just start." You'll be glad you did.

During my first one-day sprint at home with my 3-year-old son, we got games, home chores, and legitimate fun done before dinner. This tiny test proved that it's best to "just start." Start at home, start at work, start at school, start with a single project or major task. I continued using Scrum for more and more of my project work – Scrum more than doubled my capacity. I started simple, each sticky note single task was equal to a single point. My first sprints were five to eight point weeks and after six weeks I was consistently above 50 points a week without working any extra time.

Scrum changed how I worked, and the people around me noticed it. I was shortly promoted to project manager and began serving on multiple company committees. Less than two years later I became a Certified ScrumMaster®. Sutherland told me I was the first from the construction industry but wasn't surprised since even Toyota was now sending people for Scrum Master certification. Becoming Agile was one of Toyota's newest company initiatives. We spent hours talking about Lean Construction and how aligned the Scrum framework is for daily personal and team improvements. The Scrum Master role is mostly modeled from Toyota's chief engineer, and I moved *The Toyota Way* by Jeff Liker up on my reading list. That's a topic for another book.

Chapter 7

New Habits, Better Results

I smashed through my improvement plateau! I started with a velocity of less than ten change orders per sprint in my first week. In less than two years I was promoted from the project manager of a single project to national Lean Manager to serve all projects and teams across the United States of America. My final project manager sprints were above sixty points a sprint up from less than ten when I first started. That is a sixfold increase, I was finally speeding. In less than three years in that role, I earned the title of Director of Lean and became responsible to enable organization-wide continuous improvement culture by integrating our company's core values, Lean Construction principles, and methods into how we deliver projects from the project level up through supporting departments. The responsibility includes both strategy and tactics to drive and sustain local and national operational excellence objectives via business planning execution.

I upgraded my measurement methods and started tracking my velocity visually. I found that even though I was serving dozens of teams a year, people were waiting on average, almost 25 days for engagements, see figure below from late 2018.

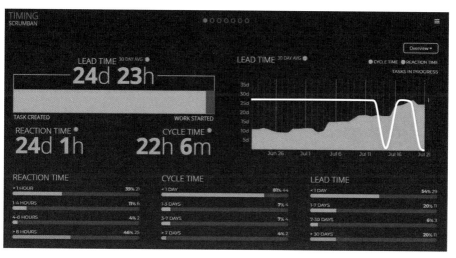

Figure 7.1

The role had exponentially expanded, and I needed to Scrum my job. As a national Lean Construction manager, I was iterating on training and coaching design and construction project teams in planning, project execution, strategic scheduling, self-perform work, and professional development across all contract types including Integrated Project Delivery, Design-Build, Lump Sum, Unit Price, Cost Plus, and Target Cost Construction Contracts. I also had to guide leaders to institute project-level risk management changes. Common construction project risks include:

- Safety: Job site hazards that can result in worker accidents/injuries.

- Financial: Negative impacts to cash flow, including delayed change orders, progress payments, unexpected cost increases, and even labor competition with other nearby projects.

- Legal: Disputes in the fulfillment of contracts deliverables with clients, contractors, and suppliers.

- Project: Job site hazards such as poor management of manpower, equipment, materials, space, methods, or even misunderstanding of project deliverables.

- Environmental: Floods, earthquakes, and other natural phenomena that damage construction sites and make work inaccessible.

The goal is to achieve positive client feedback, improve trade partner relations, and enable easier project delivery by mentoring leaders and systematically sharing best practices. I evaluated this sketch of the Scrum framework I drew after reading and re-reading the 2017 Scrum Guide looking for weak links in my Sprint cycles.

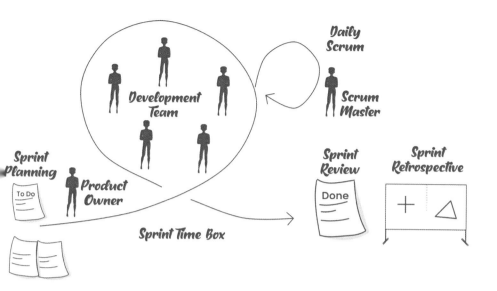

Figure 7.2

After reflection, I realized that I wasn't spending adequate time in Sprint Planning. I experimented by increasing my planning time from 20 minutes to half a day. Here are the results after two months or nearly eight Sprints.

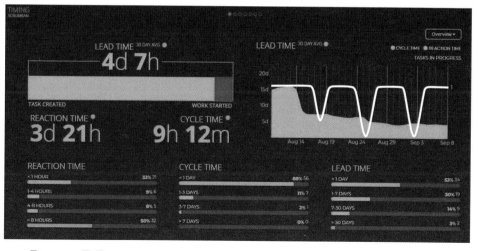

Figure 7.3

An overall lead time reduction from nearly 25 days to 5 days is a fivefold increase in throughput or flow. Not pictured in the data is my travel for project engagements. In my first year serving nationally, I worked with six project teams. In less than three years I worked with an average of 15 teams per month, mostly in person, face-to-face. In 2019, I averaged between 2-4 cities per week and the National Lean Leaders team was about 20 people strong. After COVID-19 grounded my travels in March of 2020, I iterated again and began sprinting with our Lean leaders growing the group to over 60. By late 2021, the group has grown to over 80 and continues adding Lean learders from across the country.

If you want to sprint and more than double your capacity, visit

Felipe's Trello Resources.

Click the top left card to download/read the free current Scrum Guide. My digital Scrum resources board will help you get started. It includes links to short videos that will explain Scrum in more detail. Every day, I work through the Scrum framework and even use it to teach others. It keeps me in a continuous improvement loop. It was designed to be a habitual plan-do-check-act (PDCA) for people "developing, delivering, and sustaining complex products by a single team."

So, what's happened since I discovered Scrum? Well, I changed a lot, and my velocity shows it! I've been able to use Scrum to deliver value consistently, go more than twice as fast, and yet sustain Lean practice and professional development. How fast are you going to go? My productivity increased dramatically and has done so week after week. The disciplined daily use of Scrum enables me to continuously increase my capacity and output. I continue to measure my velocity weekly and I periodically analyze my velocity looking for trends and constraints. Why is it so powerful? Since I started embracing the Scrum values and method, I have been using it as a guide when working with others.

Being inspired and taking action are not always connected. I'm not satisfied with you only learning from my examples. I want to see what is possible for you. Small changes to how you work using the Scrum framework enable new possibilities. Answer the following questions if you are struggling to start:

- 🏠 What is my problem? Start with a problem you own and influence.

- 🏠 What is my current productivity? You have a lot to offer so periodically measure and incrementally improve your output and use your learnings to help others on your team develop.

- 🏠 How will I know if I'm improving? Sustained value delivery improves work-life, overall quality, and satisfaction. Achieving a state of flow or happiness are other indicators.

In the next chapter, you will learn more about the three invisible and powerful pillars that hold up the Scrum framework.

Chapter 8
Scrum Pillars and Values

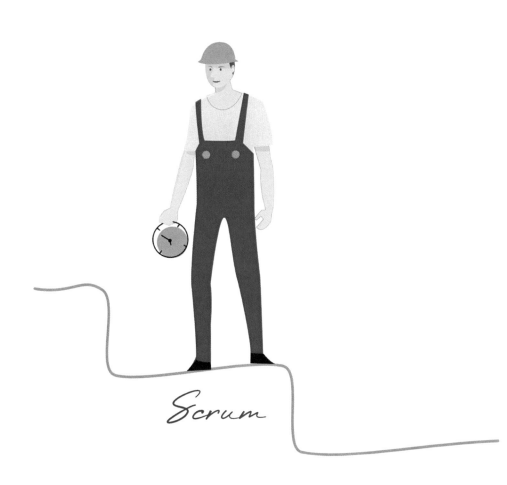

Scrum

> *"Improvement of Quality and Productivity, to be successful in any company, must be a learning process, year by year, top management leading the whole company."*

W. Edwards Deming

The Scrum framework is based on the Deming Cycle, introduced by Dr. William Edwards Deming, Plan, Do, Check/Study, Act/Adjust or more commonly known as the PDCA or PDSA cycle. This approach focuses on empirical process control theory. This means we learn by doing things, hands-on with all our senses. The actions are visible, but the learning isn't. Jeff told me he built Scrum to be an iterative experimentation framework cycle whereby teams learn by doing and have fun working.

I think of it as the scientific method adapted to fit a sequence of action steps. Experimenting in this way allows for a lightweight process for learning, doing, and gaining knowledge to improve a product or a service. The November 2017 Scrum Guide says, "Scrum makes clear the relative efficacy of your product management and work techniques so that you can continuously improve the product, the team, and the working environment." Dr. Deming made PDCA famous in his career and he learned it from his mentor, Walter Shewhart, who developed it while working at Bell Laboratories in New York. See the Scrum process framework below with PDCA overlaid.

If you are familiar with Jeff's work, you may have also heard of the OODA loop. OODA stands for Observe, Orient, Decide, and Act. You can read more about it in Chapter Eight of Jeff's book, *Scrum: The Art of Doing Twice the Work in Half the Time*. With Jeff's recommendation, I dove deeper into applying the OODA loop in business by reading *Certain to Win* by Chet Richards. The preface alone hooked me with examples from Toyota, Sun Tzu, Southwest Airlines, and numerous mentions of Lean pioneers.

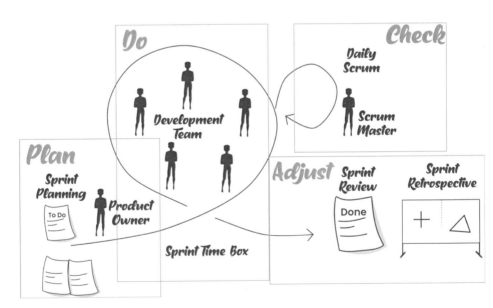

Figure 8.1

The PDCA cycle is operating invisibly inside the Scrum framework. Scrum teams begin every Sprint with the Plan step. This involves identifying the **Sprint Goal**. The goal can be met by completing an increment of the Product Backlog. The objective set by the Product Owner gives the work purpose and establishes success metrics that guide the team to self-organize the Sprint Backlog as a prioritized set of actions, **Sprint Planning.**

These **Product Backlog Item (PBI)** activities are actions for the **Do** step. The work tasks of the plan are ready to be implemented, such as designing a floor plan, coordinating trades to install in-wall utilities, or submitting a request for a proposal to win new work. Other examples of design and construction PBIs include writing contracts, completing change order work, installing a drinking fountain, selecting a building orientation, updating a budget, and other value-adding work. PBIs that are done, make progress towards the achievement of the Sprint Goal.

Each day, the **Scrum Master** guides the team through the **Daily Scrum.** This is the Check/Study step, where the team inspects their progress against the plan. Successes and problems are made visible for continuous improvement. The intent of this Check/Study is to give the team feedback via their own conversations with each other on how they are accomplishing the **Sprint Goal**. Scrum teams often identify issues as a result of the Daily Scrum meeting that are impediments worthy of targeted actions. Inspection is a key part of Scrum.

The discussions and changes resulting from the Daily Scrum meeting make a large part of the Adjust/Act step. The **Sprint Review** and Retrospective also serve to close the PDCA cycle and complete the next Act steps. The Act step integrates the team's learning generated by the whole framework which can be used to adjust the goal, change methods, or broaden the improvement cycle from small experiments to larger implementation, Product Backlog refinement or improved future Sprint Planning. The four PDCA steps repeat over and over invisibly inside the never-ending Scrum cycles fostering continuous learning and improvement.

Once you can see Scrum's underlying pattern, you'll be able to more quickly adapt the framework with any team. I want you to be able to start this no matter what your level of Lean or Agile experience is and to teach others how to deliver more value with less effort.

Scrum Pillars and Values

The 2017 Scrum Guide recommends embracing the following pillars and values to explore new ways of working with less effort and more flow. I include this commentary on the pillars and values due to the heavy influence they continue to have on my continuous improvement work and applications beyond Scrum. I use these pillars and values in other frameworks such as the Last Planner® System of Production Controls and A3 Problem-Solving. In Chapter 9, I've included the 2020 Scrum Guide update and commentary for how I'm using the updates with Scrum teams presently.

Scrum Pillars

1. **Transparency**

   "Significant aspects of the process must be visible to those responsible for the outcome. Transparency requires those aspects be defined by a common standard so observers share a common understanding of what is being seen."

Seeing the team's goals, current and future work, impediments, and speed is powerful and should not be undervalued. To make our work visible is a key principle in continuous improvement. To improve products or services, teams need to be able to visualize them first.

2. **Inspection**

"Scrum users must frequently inspect Scrum artifacts and progress toward a Sprint Goal to detect undesirable variances. Their inspection should not be so frequent that inspection gets in the way of the work. Inspections are most beneficial when diligently performed by skilled inspectors at the point of work."

One-piece flow is the goal for perfect value delivery to satisfy a customer. To fulfill the customer's expectations requires time and resources. Scrum teams need to work towards smaller batch sizes, as close to a single piece as reasonably possible, in order to get faster feedback and ensure value is delivered at each step of their process from the customer's perspective.

3. **Adaptation**

"If an inspector determines that one or more aspects of a process deviate outside acceptable limits and that the resulting product will be unacceptable, the process or the material being processed must be adjusted. An adjustment must be made as soon as possible to minimize further deviation."

There is nothing more constant than change. Time and chance

impact all experiences for individuals, teams, and businesses. Markets change, customer's needs vary, and worker's skill levels are not predictable. People and teams that can more quickly adapt have greater opportunities to match market demand with supply.

Scrum Values

The Scrum values are the foundation for a more creative, productive, and fun environment for individuals and teams. The better the collaboration, the easier it is to achieve a sustainable pace of work. I have heard many stories from construction professionals about how dreadful their work environments and relationships inside their organizations are. As I used to be in the same situation, I can relate a lot. The good news is that Scrum gave me back my life because the following values were implemented in my work environments.

1. **Openness**

   The first value is openness. Based on the pillar of transparency, we need openness to share our ideas. We want to make everything visible. We want to know the work by seeing it. We want to have any required management reporting be done automatically or with the most minimal tooling or processes. We want to hear the best ideas from everyone. Anyone needs to be able to raise an impediment, propose a solution. Anyone can put anything on the Scrum Backlog. All meetings are open to anyone to attend. Jeff worked with a congressman who implemented the Sunshine Law in the state of Colorado. It said that anybody could attend any meeting and that nothing is hidden. A foreign approach for many organizations. We need to encourage the next value to make it happen.

2. **Courage**

To pave the way for real openness, we need courageous people. This means that individuals must be willing to step up and out of their comfort zone because individual and team growth can only happen there. It's not easy to speak truth to power. It's not easy to tell management what they're doing seems wrong, that company policies are not serving the customer, and that something needs to change. The inner power needed to propose a new idea, raise an impediment, get things fixed, requires immense courage in many if not most traditional companies. Beware of the level of criticism people in your companies are facing. Unsound and illogical criticism in corporations is incredible and rampant. This is, unfortunately, our reality, and it is shocking. The solution is to teach people how to value themselves and others. That's when respect comes into play.

3. **Respect**

Respect trumps harmony all the time. This is fundamental and critically important. From systems theory we know that most organizations face problems that are not individual people's issues, they are systemic problems. Coupled with that, We also know that human beings have a tendency to blame others for their individual problems. This irrational psychology of blaming is called the fundamental attribution error. The good news is that we can learn to self-correct and overcome this tendency. Respect is not just a nice thing to do. It's crucial for leadership at all levels. In Scrum, leadership begins with the team, which is self-leading. The Scrum Master who is facilitating the team, the Product Owner, and the management of the organization, all need to practice respect with each other. When they do, they will encourage the people that create the value to speak up. And only then will new ideas flow for continuous improvement. When we enable openness, it flows from courage and respect, and that builds agreement on what we should do and how we should do it.

4. **Focus**

The previous values enable teams to focus. Think of the average experience you have had with teams. The average team is not really a team, they're actually individual people working on individual priorities. A team that can focus on a goal works together with each other to move in the right direction. Teams that don't do that will fail. We must agree on what the goal is and how people can help each other move towards it. If we can get everybody aligned, we often get at least twice the work done in half the time. In other words, we work less and have more fun. It is much easier for a team to commit to working together when there is alignment on a goal.

5. **Commitment**

Commitment is the cornerstone of Scrum. Think of teams that haven't yet decided as a group to do something. They progress slowly while uncertainty is high. When a team commits, energy flows. Some of this is obvious because once other parts of the organization see that your team is committed to a goal, communicating needs, and working to achieve it, the organization tends to help you achieve that goal. That is flow. Jeff taught me that people working in quantum mechanics drew some parallels here. When you observe an electron, for example, it starts to change. The more you observe and the more you focus, the more things change. Everything flows from that truth. We can recreate the environment that we are working in by just being committed. Where attention goes, energy flows. People bring up excuses every day why Scrum will never work in their organization. They complain that too much is broken, nothing could ever be fixed to create real flow. Scrum is designed as a tool for you to alter your environment. I have helped thousands of people turn their workplace into one where it's actually rewarding and fun to work. As a result, productivity spikes. Bye, bye scarcity, hello abundance with actions from our own hands via step-by-step, piece-by-piece, impediment-by-impediment changes, and moving things forward. According to Jeff, "Commitment is the magic of Scrum...Magic happens when the commitment of the team occurs. And it only happens with openness, courage, respect, focus, and commitment."

Key Takeaways
Part II

1. Two great patterns to increase capacity and to formulate a goal are:

   🏠 Good Housekeeping, Pattern 80

♟ The Sprint Goal, Pattern 71

2. Key questions to help you figure out whether to use Scrum

   a. What is my problem, struggle, or frustration with work right now?

   b. What is my current productivity level?

   c. Am I able to do what is needed to help deliver my projects?

   d. How will I know whether or not I am improving?

3. The 11 main steps of Scrum are:

   1) Pick a product

   2) Pick a team

   3) Pick a Scrum Master

   4) Create and prioritize Backlog Items

   5) Refine/Estimate the Backlog

   6) Sprint Planning

   7) Make work visible

   8) Daily stand-up

   9) Sprint review

   10) Sprint retrospective

   11) Repeat

4. Scrum Patterns and Values

Scrum Pillars (Transparency, Inspection, Adaptation) and Values foster creativity, innovation, and the health and wholeness of the team.

The five Scrum values are

1. Openness: Scrum events are clear and visible to everyone.

2. Courage: Be willing to step up and speak your truth.

3. Respect: for people and ideas, including those that differ from your own.

4. Focus: With focus your work becomes faster, more efficient, and better.

5. Commitment: Commit to your team, the sprint goal, and the scrum values.

In Part III you will learn how to adapt the framework and make value delivery a habit with tactical Scrum examples.

3
PART

USING THE SCRUM GUIDE TO MAKE YOUR PLAYBOOK

Chapter 9

Using the Scrum Guide to Make Your Playbook

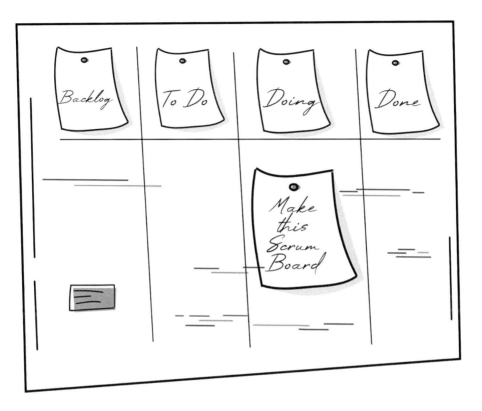

Figure 9.1

It is time to begin using what we know. If you have never Sprinted before, don't worry! Let's go slow together to go fast. The above Scrum board is just one example and has everything we need to start. A new Scrum Master may include this type of Scrum board and tasks with a new team to get started. Here are some cards you might want on your board.

Backlog (Product Backlog)	To Do (Sprint Backlog)	Doing	Done
As a new Scrum user, I want to use Scrum daily for a month so that I can make it a habit.	Watch this video from Scrum Inc. Intro to the Scrum Framework 		

Table 8.1

Only do one thing at a time. Move your sticky notes into the 'Doing' column only when you are actively working on that task. People really work on one task at a time, moving stickies to the 'Done' column when that task is completed, one by one. Multitasking is a myth. If you think you are good at it, keep thinking about it while you read these words. Google "Dual Task Interference" or "Context Switching" if you don't believe me. Save yourself from wasting any more of your time, run an experiment to see how much faster it is to work on a single thing at a time. Now we can read the official framework adapted for construction to get into the game.

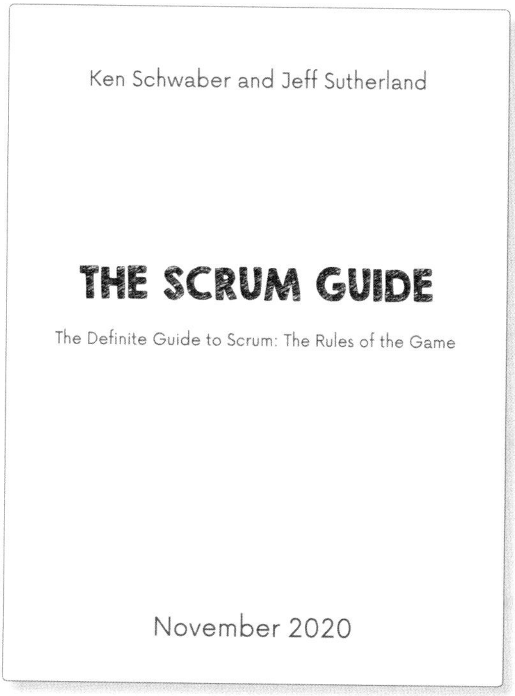
Ken Schwaber and Jeff Sutherland

THE SCRUM GUIDE

The Definite Guide to Scrum: The Rules of the Game

November 2020

Image 8.1

I highly recommend you read the current Scrum Guide right now before starting the next paragraph. At the time of this publication, I used the 2020 Scrum Guide that was published in November 2020. It is free forever and available in over 30 languages online.

On the following pages, you will find original excerpts from the Scrum Guide with content added to help design and construction professionals adopt Scrum in their daily work

Purpose of the Scrum Guide

Figure 8.2

We [Jeff Sutherland and Ken Schwaber] developed Scrum in the early 1990s. We wrote this version of the first Scrum guide in 2010 to help people worldwide understand Scrum. We have evolved the Guide since then through small, functional updates. Together we stand behind it.

The Scrum Guide contains the definition of Scrum. Each element of the framework serves a specific purpose that is essential to the overall value and results realized with Scrum. Changing the core design or ideas of

Scrum, leaving out elements, or not following the rules of Scrum, covers up problems and limits the benefits of Scrum, potentially even rendering it useless.

Using sticky notes on a board with "To Do," "Doing," and "Done" columns isn't enough to be Scrum and not even enough to be considered Kanban.

We follow the growing use of Scrum within an ever-growing complex world. We are humbled to see Scrum being adopted in many domains holding essentially complex work, beyond software product development where Scrum has its roots. As Scrum's use spreads, developers, researchers, analysts, scientists, and other specialists do the work. We use the word "developers" in Scrum not to exclude, but to simplify. If you get value from Scrum, consider yourself included.

The usage of Scrum has spread far beyond hardware, software, and information technology. It is also being used by students, educators, bankers, business startups, fortune 500 companies, and design and construction professionals around the globe. I will be using "project team" or "team member" instead of "developers."

As Scrum is being used, patterns, processes, and insights that fit the Scrum framework as described in this document, may be found, applied and devised. Their description is beyond the purpose of the Scrum Guide because they are context sensitive and differ widely between Scrum uses. Such tactics for using within the Scrum framework vary widely and are described elsewhere.

This book includes many examples and there are even more applications described on my podcast, The EBFC Show. How Scrum is used by teams even inside the same project can differ widely since tactics for using the Scrum framework will vary based on the team's work capabilities and Scrum experience.

Scrum Definition

Scrum is a lightweight framework that helps teams and organizations generate value through adaptive solutions for complex problems.

According to Jeff Scrum provides the minimum sized amount of bureaucracy to allow people to work together to deliver owner value.

In a nutshell, Scrum requires a Scrum Master to foster an environment where:

1. A Product Owner orders the work for a complex problem into a Product Backlog.

2. The Scrum Team turns a selection of the work into an Increment of value during a Sprint.

3. The Scrum Team and its stakeholders inspect the results and adjust for the next Sprint.

4. Repeat

The "Product Owner" is a functional title. It is for the person responsible for what the Scrum team delivers. In construction, it is most often the person on the team that can allocate resources and most often interfaces with the project owner and sets priorities to support meeting the owner's needs/expectations. An increment of value is exactly equivalent to installed work in place for the construction phase or completed design drawings/details/calculations for the preconstruction phase.

Scrum is simple. Try it as is and determine if its philosophy, theory, and structure help to achieve goals and create value. The Scrum framework is purposefully incomplete, only defining the parts required to implement Scrum theory. Scrum is built upon by the collective intelligence of the people using it. Rather than provide people with detailed instructions, the rules of Scrum guide their relationships and interactions.

Just try it. I wasn't perfect when I started but I was patient and disciplined. Today I've helped thousands of teams get started for themselves while delivering value daily for my partners.

Various processes, techniques and methods can be employed within the framework. Scrum wraps around existing practices or renders them unnecessary. Scrum makes visible the relative efficacy of current management, environment, and work techniques, so that improvements can be made.

Scrum is a framework that can support and enable many types of project team organizations and Lean tools like the Last Planner® System of Production Controls, project processes like onboarding, inspections, planning and scheduling, change orders, change management, and countless other applications.

Scrum Theory

Scrum is founded on empiricism and lean thinking.

I have confirmed with dozens of experts across the globe including people working at the Lean Enterprise Institute that were part of bringing the word "lean" into our vocabulary and have confirmed it should not be capitalized. Just some fun lean trivia.

Empiricism asserts that knowledge comes from experience and making decisions based on what is observed. Lean thinking reduces waste and focuses on the essentials.

Scrum employs an iterative, incremental approach to optimize predictability and to control risk. Scrum engages groups of people who collectively have all the skills and expertise to do the work and share or acquire such skills as needed.

Iteration is aligned with design thinking, continuous improvement, and Scrum is built upon the scientific method/cycle of PDCA - Plan, Do, Check/Study, Act/Adjust

Scrum combines four formal events [meetings] for inspection and adaptation within a containing event, the Sprint. These events work because they implement the empirical Scrum pillars of transparency, inspection, and adaptation.

Transparency

The emergent process and work must be visible to those performing the work as well as those receiving the work. With Scrum, important decisions are based on the perceived state of its three formal artifacts. Artifacts that have low transparency can lead to decisions that diminish value and increase risk.

Increasing transparency of the work done by project teams is one of the greatest improvement changes that will nearly magically boost many key performance indicators from team health, safety, quality, schedule, and cost.

Transparency enables inspection. Inspection without transparency is misleading and wasteful.

Waste is a crime against humanity and should be minimized and eliminated. See the chapter on "Six Lean Construction Principles" for how to recognize and banish waste.

Inspection

The Scrum artifacts [things we can see and touch] and the progress toward agreed goals must be inspected frequently and diligently to detect potentially undesirable variances or problems. To help with inspection, Scrum provides cadence in the form of its five events.

Inspection enables adaptation. Inspection without adaptation is considered pointless. Scrum events are designed to provoke change.

Design and construction projects are ripe with change. A typical project experiences changes in scope, variation in skill level among trades and management alike, changes in weather, coordination changes, etc.

Adaptation

If any aspects of a process deviate outside acceptable limits or if the resulting product is unacceptable, the process being applied or the materials being produced must be adjusted. The adjustment must be made as soon as possible to minimize further deviation.

Variation is guaranteed to occur, be open with yourself and your team about changes.

Adaptation becomes more difficult when the people involved are not empowered or self-managing. A Scrum Team is expected to adapt the moment it learns anything new through inspection.

A new Scrum team doesn't start off empowered or self-managing, it may take more than a handful of sprints before the team begins to exhibit autonomous adaptation to changes.

Scrum Values

Successful use of Scrum depends on people becoming more proficient in living the five Scrum values: Commitment, Focus, Openness, Respect, and Courage.

Failure to deeply understand and use these values will prevent you from actually doing real Scrum.

The Scrum Team commits to achieving its goals and to supporting each other. Their primary focus is on the work of the Sprint to make the best possible progress toward these goals. The Scrum Team and its stakeholders are open about the work and the challenges. Scrum Team members respect each other to be capable, independent people, and are respected as such by the people with whom they work. The Scrum Team members have the courage to do the right thing, to work on tough problems.

These values lead to higher team performance and prevent typical team dysfunctions such as low trust and low engagement.

These values give direction to the Scrum Team with regard to their work, actions, and behavior. The decisions that are made, the steps taken, and the way Scrum is used should reinforce these values, not diminish or undermine them. The Scrum Team members learn and explore the values as they work with the Scrum events and artifacts. When these values are embodied by the Scrum Team and the people they work with, the empirical Scrum pillars of transparency, inspection, and adaptation come to life building trust.

Scrum Team

The fundamental unit of Scrum is a small team of people, a Scrum Team. The Scrum Team consists of one Scrum Master [team captain as commonly used in EduScrum], one Product Owner [not a project manager by default], and Developers [team members/project partners]. Within a Scrum Team, there are no sub-teams or hierarchies. It is a cohesive unit of professionals focused on one objective at a time, the Product Goal.

Scrum Teams are cross-functional, meaning the members have all the skills necessary to create value each Sprint. They are also self-managing, meaning they internally decide who does what, when, and how.

The Scrum Team is small enough to remain nimble and large enough to complete significant work within a Sprint, typically 10 or fewer people. In general, we have found that smaller teams communicate better and are more productive.

Teams of 4-6 are exponentially faster than teams of 10. Larger teams have more communication channels, and workflow stops when communication stops. Refer back to the Good Housekeeping Pattern for examples of wasted energy and time when team members can't see the current progress of their work or don't have access to needed information.

If Scrum Teams become too large, they should consider reorganizing into multiple cohesive Scrum Teams, each focused on the same product. Therefore, they should share the same Product Goal, Product Backlog, and Product Owner.

The Scrum Team is responsible for all product-related activities from stakeholder collaboration, verification, maintenance, operation, experimentation, research and development, and anything else that might be required. They are structured and empowered by the organization to manage their own work. Working in Sprints at a sustainable pace improves the Scrum Team's focus and consistency.

The entire Scrum Team is accountable for creating a valuable, useful Increment every Sprint.

Typical construction projects deliver incremental work in place each month and receive payments for the whole project based on progress to date. This is identically an increment of value delivery. Smaller increments allow for faster feedback and opportunities for greater value delivery.

Scrum defines three specific accountabilities within the Scrum Team: the Developers, the Product Owner, and the Scrum Master.

Developers

Developers are the people in the Scrum Team that are committed to creating any aspect of a usable Increment for each Sprint.

I encourage Scrum team members to call themselves team members or project partners. Jeff Sutherland has repeatedly said in many of his talks that the functions of the role are more important than the role label.

The specific skills needed by the Developers are often broad and will vary with the domain of work. However, the Developers are always accountable for:

- Creating a plan for the Sprint, the Sprint Backlog;

- Instilling quality by adhering to a Definition of Done;

- Adapting their plan each day toward the Sprint Goal; and,

- Holding each other accountable as professionals.

Product Owner

The Product Owner is accountable for maximizing the value of the product resulting from the work of the Scrum Team. How this is done may vary widely across organizations, Scrum Teams, and individuals.

Product Owners in design and construction projects are the single person typically most responsible for the project's revenue flows, profit margins, and team assignments. A cross functional design team may have the lead architect serve in the product owner role. An engineering team may have the engineering manager or director of engineering serve as the product owner. A small construction project team may have the project manager serve as the product owner. Larger construction projects may have a project executive or project director serve as the product owner. In the field, project superintendents or foremen often best fit the role for product owners.

The Product Owner is also accountable for effective Product Backlog management, which includes:

- Developing and explicitly communicating the Product Goal;

- Creating and clearly communicating Product Backlog items;

- Ordering Product Backlog items; and,

- Ensuring that the Product Backlog is transparent, visible and understood.

The Product Owner may do the above work or may delegate the responsibility to others. Regardless, the Product Owner remains accountable.

For Product Owners to succeed, the entire organization must respect their decisions. These decisions are visible in the content and ordering of the Product Backlog, and through the inspectable Increment at the Sprint Review.

The Product Owner is one person, not a committee. The Product Owner may represent the needs of many stakeholders in the Product Backlog. Those wanting to change the Product Backlog can do so by trying to convince the Product Owner.

Product Owners very often also pull product backlog items meaning that they work as part of the team, they are responsible for what the team delivers each sprint.

Scrum Master

The Scrum Master is accountable for establishing Scrum as defined in the Scrum Guide. They do this by helping everyone understand Scrum theory and practice, both within the Scrum Team and the organization.

The Scrum Master is accountable for the Scrum Team's effectiveness. They do this by enabling the Scrum Team to improve its practices, within the Scrum framework.

Scrum Masters are true leaders who serve the Scrum Team and the larger organization.

Scrum Masters very often also pull product backlog items meaning that they work as part of the team, they are responsible for enabling the team to use Scrum and improve the team's performance each sprint.

The Scrum Master serves the Scrum Team in several ways, including:

- Coaching the team members in self-management and cross-functionality;

- Helping the Scrum Team focus on creating high-value Increments that meet the Definition of Done;

- Causing the removal of impediments [bottlenecks/constraints/issues/challenges] to the Scrum Team's progress; and,

- Ensuring that all Scrum events take place and are positive, productive, and kept within the timebox.

The Scrum Master serves the Product Owner in several ways, including:

- Helping find techniques for effective Product Goal definition and Product Backlog management;

- Helping the Scrum Team understand the need for clear and concise Product Backlog items;

- Helping establish empirical product planning for a complex environment; and,

- Facilitating stakeholder collaboration as requested or needed.

The Scrum Master serves the organization in several ways, including:

- Leading, training, and coaching the organization in its Scrum adoption;

- Planning and advising Scrum implementations within the organization;

- Helping employees and stakeholders understand and enact an empirical approach for complex work; and,

- Removing barriers between stakeholders and Scrum Teams.

Scrum Events

The Sprint is a container for all other events. Each event in Scrum is a formal opportunity to inspect and adapt Scrum artifacts. These events are specifically designed to enable the transparency required. Failure to operate any events as prescribed results in lost opportunities to inspect and adapt. Events are used in Scrum to create regularity and to minimize the need for meetings not defined in Scrum.

Optimally, all events are held at the same time and place to reduce complexity.

The Sprint

Sprints are the heartbeat of Scrum, where ideas are turned into value.

They are fixed length events of one month or less to create consistency. A new Sprint starts immediately after the conclusion of the previous Sprint.

General contractors often use one week sprint durations. Preconstruction and estimating teams often use single week sprint durations as well. Design teams typically use shorter duration sprints when design is emerging and shift to longer sprint durations when they enter into production design (detailed design). Field teams composed of tradespeople often use single week duration sprints. Once a team picks a duration, keep it for at least three sprints before deciding to experiment with another. This will allow the team to inspect and adapt to shorter or longer sprint durations. The better practice is to maintain the same sprint duration for the entire span of a project's life cycle. I have personally used single week sprints successfully for years. My podcast team uses a two week sprint cycle, new shows post every two weeks. I've seen large multi-hundred million dollar construction teams successfully use four week sprint cycles and later shift to weekly sprints as they learn to decrease the batch size of their work increments. It is quite counterintuitive but smaller batch sizes deliver faster than large batch sizes due to the longer wait times from one phase of work to the next.

All the work necessary to achieve the Product Goal, including Sprint Planning, Daily Scrums, Sprint Review, and Sprint Retrospective, happen within Sprints.

During the Sprint:

- No changes are made that would endanger the Sprint Goal;

- Quality does not decrease;

- The Product Backlog is refined as needed; and,

- Scope may be clarified and renegotiated with the Product Owner as more is learned.

Sprints enable predictability by ensuring inspection and adaptation of progress toward a Product Goal at least every calendar month. When a Sprint's horizon is too long the Sprint Goal may become invalid, complexity may rise, and risk may increase. Shorter Sprints can be employed to generate more learning cycles and limit risk of cost and effort to a smaller time frame. Each Sprint may be considered a short project.

Various practices exist to forecast progress, like burn-downs, burn-ups, or cumulative flows. While proven useful, these do not replace the importance of empiricism. In complex environments, what will happen is unknown.

All phases of design and construction projects qualify as complex since they consist of many different and interconnected parts. A team should focus on the Sprint Goal to deliver value first before expending energy on forecasting. Let the team get through at least three sprints before you can reasonably start to predict how fast they are going to deliver.

Only what has already happened may be used for forward-looking decision making.

A Sprint could be canceled if the Sprint Goal becomes obsolete. Only the Product Owner has the authority to cancel the Sprint.

Cancelling sprints is not good for team morale so weigh the decision carefully.

Sprint Planning

Sprint Planning initiates the Sprint by laying out the work to be performed for the Sprint. This resulting plan is created by the collaborative work of the entire Scrum Team.

The Product Owner ensures that attendees are prepared to discuss the most important Product Backlog items and how they map to the Product Goal. The Scrum Team may also invite other people to attend Sprint Planning to provide advice. [Examples may include facility personnel, doctors, nurses, students, faculty, other design disciplines, trade partners, inspectors, etc.]

Sprint Planning addresses the following topics:

Topic One: Why is this Sprint valuable?

> The Product Owner proposes how the product [service or combination of both] could increase its value and utility in the current Sprint. The whole Scrum Team then collaborates to define a Sprint Goal that communicates why the Sprint is valuable to stakeholders. The Sprint Goal must be finalized prior to the end

of Sprint Planning.

Topic Two: What can be done this Sprint?

Through discussion with the Product Owner, the Developers select items from the Product Backlog to include in the current Sprint. The Scrum Team may refine these items during this process, which increases understanding and confidence.

Selecting how much can be completed within a Sprint may be challenging. However, the more the Developers know about their past performance, their upcoming capacity, and their Definition of Done, the more confident they will be in their Sprint forecasts.

Topic Three: How will the chosen work get done?

For each selected Product Backlog item, the Developers plan the work necessary to create an Increment that meets the Definition of Done. This is often done by decomposing Product Backlog items into smaller work items of one day or less. How this is done is at the sole discretion of the Developers. No one else tells them how to turn Product Backlog items into Increments of value.

The Sprint Goal, the Product Backlog items selected for the Sprint, plus the plan for delivering them are together referred to as the Sprint Backlog [also commonly known as the "To Do" list of work tasks].

Sprint Planning is timeboxed to a maximum of eight hours for a one-month Sprint. For shorter Sprints, the event is usually shorter.

Several times during a given project of multiple years duration, I've increased the Sprint Planning time and achieved greater output of value delivery. I often spend a few hours or more in Sprint Planning with new teams working on one week sprints and as they experience Scrum more, the planning time decreases to about two hours or less each sprint. Ben Franklin famously said, "If you fail to plan, you are planning to fail."

Daily Scrum

The purpose of the Daily Scrum is to inspect progress toward the Sprint Goal and adapt the Sprint Backlog as necessary, adjusting the upcoming planned work.

The Developers can select whatever structure and techniques they want, as long as their Daily Scrum focuses on progress toward the Sprint Goal and produces an actionable plan for the next day of work. This creates focus and improves self-management.

The Daily Scrum is a 15-minute event [meeting/daily standup/daily huddle] for the Developers of the Scrum Team. To reduce complexity, it is held at the same time and place every working day of the Sprint. If the Product Owner or Scrum Master are actively working on items in the Sprint Backlog, they participate as Developers.

> More than 99.9% of Scrum teams have the Product Owners and Scrum Master work on Sprint Backlog items. Better Scrum Masters start by facilitating the Daily Scrum and quickly enable all team members to take turns and keep them engaging.

> Construction jobsite teams start or end the team's day with the Daily Scrum. This purposeful meeting structure will facilitate more efficient communication, collaboration, and personal

accountability. The following sections are better practice and based on decades of direct participation and observation.

The Who

The trades put in the work that builds the building. When they see that the entire team is active in the Daily Scrum, it fosters greater buy-in. Team members for construction often include foremen, assistant superintendents, general foremen, and superintendents. Meetings will be even more productive if the general contractor's project manager, assistant project manager, and project engineers attend. Their participation provides faster resolutions on constraints that may involve the input of the design team or owner.

15-Minutes or Less

The meeting is always fifteen minutes or less. Period. Some teams use a phone timer to practice keeping it short and sweet.

No Distractions

Everyone participates with full engagement. Allowing participants to use their phones, tablets, or computers communicates the wrong message of mutual respect. Effective person-to-person communication is the focus, not browsing devices.

Stand Up

Remove the chairs from the meeting space or be at the team's Scrum board with everyone standing. This drives engagement and focus.

Set and Keep the Standard

Each team member completes the following statements:

- 🏠 Yesterday I worked on...

- 🏠 Today I'm working on...with X crews and Y workers on-site.

- 🏠 My task constraints/needs are...

- 🏠 I'm expecting these Z material deliveries at...

These statements engage the field leaders running the work. Sharing these project updates increases collaboration and coordination with others.

No Problem-Solving

The meeting identifies problems, which end up in the Parking Lot to be resolved with responsible parties after the meeting. Parking Lots use whiteboards to capture issues as they arise so that they are visible for everyone and keep the meeting flow uninterrupted. Placing items in the parking lot means that a quick discussion follows the huddle with the affected people to discuss the issues or circumstances that did not require everyone's involvement.

Daily Scrums improve communications, identify impediments, promote quick decision-making, and consequently eliminate the need for other meetings.

If you are asking yourself where to begin with Scrum, the Daily Scrum is often a great starting point that improves teamwork, increases capacity, and helps enable work to flow more effortlessly.

The Daily Scrum is not the only time Developers are allowed to adjust their plan. They often meet throughout the day for more detailed discussions about adapting or re-planning the rest of the Sprint's work.

We are engaged in complex work, replanning and negotiating changes to the work are normal and should be expected. If you aren't convinced, examine any waterfall, Ghantt chart, critical path schedule to see how the initial project plan matched the final as-built project plan.

Sprint Review

The purpose of the Sprint Review is to inspect the outcome of the Sprint and determine future adaptations. The Scrum Team presents the results of their work to key stakeholders and progress toward the Product Goal is discussed.

In design, this is often done as a meeting where stakeholders see completed portions of the design and give feedback. Better practice is for the team to record all the feedback and only ask clarifying questions, not engage in defending the design or arguing. In construction, this is often done by inspecting the completed work in place, aka job walk. Think of how teams review construction mockups for some inspiration.

During the event, the Scrum Team and stakeholders review what was accomplished in the Sprint and what has changed in their environment. Based on this information, attendees collaborate on what to do next. The Product Backlog may also be adjusted to meet new opportunities. The Sprint Review is a working session and the Scrum Team should avoid limiting it to a presentation.

The Sprint Review is the second to last event of the Sprint and is timeboxed to a maximum of four hours for a one-month Sprint. For shorter Sprints, the event is usually shorter.

The math works out to be about 60 minutes of review time for each week of a Sprint. A two week Sprint would allocate a two hour Sprint Review.

Sprint Retrospective

The purpose of the Sprint Retrospective is to plan ways to increase quality and effectiveness.

This meeting is only for the Scrum team, no outside stakeholders. It is a meeting for the team to reflect and find improvements to experiment with on the next Sprint.

The Scrum Team inspects how the last Sprint went with regards to individuals, interactions, processes, tools, and their Definition of Done. Inspected elements often vary with the domain of work. Assumptions that led them astray are identified and their origins explored. The Scrum Team discusses what went well during the Sprint, what problems it encountered, and how those problems were (or were not) solved.

Experienced Lean Construction team members may even use A3 Problem-Solving or Value Stream Mapping tools to aid in problem solving.

The Scrum Team identifies the most helpful changes to improve its effectiveness. The most impactful improvements are addressed as soon as possible. They may even be added to the Sprint Backlog for the next Sprint.

The Sprint Retrospective concludes the Sprint. It is timeboxed to a maximum of three hours for a one-month Sprint. For shorter Sprints, the event is usually shorter.

When a new Scrum team is starting out, plan for a three hour retro, you can always end a meeting early when you accomplish its purpose. Incredible innovation ideas typically emerge from these meetings that help teams accelerate with less effort in subsequent Sprints.

Scrum Artifacts

Scrum's artifacts represent work or value. They are designed to maximize transparency of key information. Thus, everyone inspecting them has the same basis for adaptation.

Artifacts are objects we use during the Sprints, such as Scrum boards, drawing sheets, work in place, photos, etc.

Each artifact contains a commitment to ensure it provides information that enhances transparency and focus against which progress can be measured:

- For the Product Backlog it is the Product Goal.

  The project goal answers the big "Why" as to the purpose or intention of the complete construction project.

- For the Sprint Backlog it is the Sprint Goal.

  See the Scrum Patterns section for more detail on the Sprint Goal Pattern.

🔲 For the Increment it is the Definition of Done.

In design, the product is a design or part of design such as exterior elevation drawings or a systems line diagram. In construction, the product is the project or part of the project such as corridor drywall framing or incremental phase of work such as backfilling a portion of the site.

These commitments exist to reinforce empiricism and the Scrum values for the Scrum Team and their stakeholders.

Product Backlog

The Product Backlog is an emergent, ordered list of what the team needs to improve the product. It is the single source of work undertaken by the Scrum Team.

Product Backlog items that can be Done by the Scrum Team within one Sprint are deemed ready for selection in a Sprint Planning event. They usually acquire this degree of transparency after refining activities. Product Backlog refinement is the act of breaking down and further defining Product Backlog items into smaller more precise items. This is an ongoing activity to add details, such as a description, order, and size. Attributes often vary with the domain of work.

In design and construction, Product Backlog items could initially be something like this:

🔲 Construction Project Team Member Onboarding

🔲 Final Building Subcontractor Contracting

🔲 Architect and Mechanical Engineer Design Coordination

The team prepares these items for an upcoming Sprint by using the Story Slicing techniques:

- **Construction Project Team Member Onboarding**

  As a new construction project team member, I can access the latest training material and best practices onsite and online so I can use the best practices. New partners will start helping the team today. New project members should complete onboarding and initial employment documentation with the project admin in a single workday. They will know why we are building this project, have all their questions answered, and meet key staff while touring the project office and site, knowing who to ask for what and where to find how-to videos and procedures.

- **Final Building Subcontractor Contracting**

  As a construction team project manager, I want the most qualified and best-priced final building cleaning contract to turn over an immaculate building to the owner at occupancy. Confirm budgeted contract value, schedule, and start date. Contract department and project director approval before draft terms are issued to the potential subcontractor. The approved contract is signed, filed, and contacts are scheduled for the first installation meeting.

- **Architect and Mechanical Engineer Design Coordination**

  As the lead project architect, I want to coordinate floor plans with mechanical room shafts and structural elements to minimize walking distances for healthcare workers while maximizing line of sight for charge nurses towards patient rooms. Resolve all inter-disciplinary conflicts. No open clouded comments remain on drawing sheets. Floor plans are conflict free, all notes resolved by priority floor, level one to level four before the next scheduled milestone date.

The Developers who will be doing the work are responsible for the sizing. The Product Owner may influence the Developers by helping them understand and select trade-offs.

Commitment: Product Goal

The Product Goal describes a future state of the product which can serve as a target for the Scrum Team to plan against. The Product Goal is in the Product Backlog. The rest of the Product Backlog emerges to define "what" will fulfill the Product Goal.

A product is a vehicle to deliver value. It has a clear boundary, known stakeholders, well-defined users or customers. A product could be a service, a physical product, or something more abstract.

In this Scrum Guide, product means product/service or combination of both.

The Product Goal is the long-term objective for the Scrum Team. They must fulfill (or abandon) one objective before taking on the next.

Sprint Backlog [To Do list of tasks]

The Sprint Backlog is composed of the Sprint Goal (why), the set of Product Backlog items selected for the Sprint (what), as well as an actionable plan for delivering the Increment (how).

Use caution, most typically I see new teams and Scrum practitioners, me included, take on too many tasks into their first Sprint. You and the team can always pull in more tasks from the top of the prioritized Product Backlog.

The Sprint Backlog is a plan by and for the Developers. It is a highly visible, real-time picture of the work that the Developers plan to accomplish during the Sprint in order to achieve the Sprint Goal. Consequently, the Sprint Backlog is updated throughout the Sprint as more is learned. It should have enough detail that they can inspect their progress in the Daily Scrum.

Well understood work typically has historical data or a budget of time, effort, and costs to accomplish the task. Use your judgement and experience of the team to make a realistic plan that will allow for smooth work progress to flow towards completion.

Commitment: Sprint Goal

The Sprint Goal is the single objective for the Sprint. Although the Sprint Goal is a commitment by the Developers, it provides flexibility in terms of the exact work needed to achieve it. The Sprint Goal also creates coherence and focus, encouraging the Scrum Team to work together rather than on separate initiatives.

Refer to the Scrum Patterns, Sprint Goal, for more details of why and how this impacts the team and aids in planning and replanning of work.

The Sprint Goal is created during the Sprint Planning event and then added to the Sprint Backlog. As the Developers work during the

Sprint, they keep the Sprint Goal in mind. If the work turns out to be different than they expected, they collaborate with the Product Owner to negotiate the scope of the Sprint Backlog within the Sprint without affecting the Sprint Goal.

Increment

An Increment is a concrete stepping stone toward the Product Goal. Each Increment is additive to all prior Increments and thoroughly verified, ensuring that all Increments work together. In order to provide value, the Increment must be usable.

Just as completing project milestones gets the team closer to final project delivery, so are increments of work in Scrum.

Multiple Increments may be created within a Sprint. The sum of the Increments is presented at the Sprint Review thus supporting empiricism. However, an Increment may be delivered to stakeholders prior to the ond of thc Sprint. The Sprint Review should never be considered a gate to releasing value.

Work cannot be considered part of an Increment unless it meets the Definition of Done.

The Scrum team uses the Sprint Goal to include and exclude what is a part of the current Increment.

Commitment: Definition of Done

The Definition of Done is a formal description of the state of the Increment when it meets the quality measures required for the product.

The moment a Product Backlog item meets the Definition of Done, an Increment is born.

Done means the customer can beneficially use the work as intended or the next partner in the value stream can add their work to the project.

The Definition of Done creates transparency by providing everyone a shared understanding of what work was completed as part of the Increment. If a Product Backlog item does not meet the Definition of Done, it cannot be released or even presented at the Sprint Review. Instead, it returns to the Product Backlog for future consideration.

If the Definition of Done for an increment is part of the standards of the organization, all Scrum Teams must follow it as a minimum. If it is not an organizational standard, the Scrum Team must create a Definition of Done appropriate for the product.

Most design and construction professionals know what level of quality and completeness is required for subsequent hand-offs in the value stream. Don't guess what is required for a given increment, ask questions, and find out during Sprint Planning.

The Developers are required to conform to the Definition of Done. If there are multiple Scrum Teams working together on a product, they must mutually define and comply with the same Definition of Done.

End Note

Scrum is free and offered in this Guide. The Scrum framework, as outlined herein, is immutable. While implementing only parts of Scrum is possible, the result is not Scrum. Scrum exists only in its entirety and functions well as a container for other techniques, methodologies, and practices.

I personally use the Scrum framework when using the Last Planner System™ of Production Controls. That is a pull system that is a collaborative, commitment-based, planning system that integrates should-can-will-did-learn conversations to make more reliable promises and project delivery.

Acknowledgements

People

Of the thousands of people who have contributed to Scrum, we should single out those who were instrumental at the start: Jeff Sutherland worked with Jeff McKenna and John Scumniotales, and Ken Schwaber worked with Mike Smith and Chris Martin, and all of them worked together. Many others contributed in the ensuing years and without their help Scrum would not be refined as it is today.

Scrum Guide History

Ken Schwaber and Jeff Sutherland first co-presented Scrum at the OOPSLA Conference in 1995. It essentially documented the learning that Ken and Jeff gained over the previous few years and made public the first formal definition of Scrum.

The Scrum Guide documents Scrum as developed, evolved, and sustained for 30-plus years by Jeff Sutherland and Ken Schwaber. Other sources provide patterns, processes, and insights that complement the Scrum framework. These may increase productivity, value, creativity, and satisfaction with the results.

The complete history of Scrum is described elsewhere. To honor the first places where it was tried and proven, we recognize Individual Inc., Newspage, Fidelity Investments, and IDX (now GE Medical).

APPLYING
THE SCRUM
FRAMEWORK

Chapter 10
Applying the Scrum Framework

Draw a building and frame it. Everything inside is scope, everything outside is Not in Contract (NIC), and put in a gate at the entrance to let change and adaptation come through. This analogy applies to beginning your individual or team Scrum. Be fully aware that your team won't high five and fist bump you when you tell them that you want to adopt Scrum. Let's look at realistic obstacles that you need to be aware of when beginning to apply the framework.

So, why would design and construction teams not use Scrum? Well, one reason could be that they never heard of the Scrum framework. I worked half my construction career before becoming aware of it. Another reason is that they are aware of it but simply don't use it because they are resistant to change or have abandoned it because of negative experiences. Some design and construction professionals even discourage Scrum adoption. I'm sharing my experiences so you can decide what is best for your teams.

Awareness Is the Key to Scrum Success

Some teams that discontinued using Scrum shared experiences about how their manager wasn't on board or how they stopped using it because the sticky notes were taking too much time to fill in and move across the Scrum board. Others told me they stopped using a specific Scrum software because it was too time-consuming to enter and update the tasks.

Further dialogue with these construction professionals revealed the real root causes:

- Individual Awareness

- Team Awareness

◆ Organization Awareness

The types of awareness with new or "experienced" design and construction Scrum teams varies. These are my summarized observations with thousands of practitioners.

1. Individual Awareness

Individuals with unreliable Scrum results can't describe the framework and are very often unaware of the existence of the Scrum Guide. Although the Scrum Guide is not a detailed procedure manual, the first section notes that tactics for implementing Scrum are described elsewhere. Individual awareness of the Scrum artifacts is also low or nonexistent. The three artifacts are: Product Backlog, Sprint Backlog, and Increment and each represents the work in three distinct phases. The key purpose of each artifact is to provide information for shared understanding of the work and progress towards the goal.

2. Team Awareness

Teams with unreliable Scrum experiences don't operate as a Scrum team. There are only three roles in Scrum: Product Owner, Scrum Master, and Development Team. Those role labels were born in software development but the Scrum Guide details how they are implemented in a variety of organizations including those with teams developing software, hardware, networks, autonomous vehicles, education, government, marketing, managing the operation of organizations, daily life management, and even for organizational knowledge transfer. Teams of people with varied titles and functions use Scrum for products, services, and organizational management. Regardless of industry, Scrum teams designate people to each of the three Scrum roles. Teams not operating in the framework are usually unaware of the roles and their unique purposes.

3. Organization Awareness

Organizations with unreliable Scrum experiences are composed of individuals, teams, or combinations of both that don't operate using the Scrum framework. Remember, collections of individuals and teams make up an organization.

In the next chapter you will learn what others have been able to do using Scrum.

Chapter 11

Construction Scrum Case Studies

The following examples serve to illuminate how Scrum helps teams overcome project problems and outline various applications of the framework. These are proven Scrum applications that involve a mix of companies, organizations, teams, and individuals. The main purpose of these case studies is to provide practical real-life applications of Scrum. Keep in mind that the actual implementation of the solution depends on complex factors. The world today is very volatile, and what is true today might not necessarily be true tomorrow, however, each of these examples started small and then scaled up.

Team doubles output without extra effort

A construction team of seven used the Scrum framework to manage all their project management tasks on a large healthcare patient bed tower project while simultaneously managing up to six smaller projects ranging in size from half a million to several million dollars. Equally impressive was the positive client feedback about the project's high quality, beneficial impact to their ongoing patient care operations, and project stakeholder collaboration among the hospital staff, designers, and frontline trade partners. From my perspective, the most impressive part of this Scrum team aside from the client feedback was that they didn't have to add more staff as more projects were added and also didn't have to work longer hours to get the work done. The team more than doubled their output without extra effort.

Team organizes record-breaking national conference in a third of the time

In 2019, I worked with a team that was geographically spread across the United States and had the task of organizing a national construction conference. Traditionally, the team (made up of construction professionals) used to take twelve months to organize the event. With Scrum, they were able to organize the event in four months and spend additional meeting time making value-added changes to the proceedings. The time saving of eight months represents 66.7% of the former 12-month duration. The event had record breaking attendance and higher customer satisfaction ratings as compared to past conferences. Often, the first big gains are reductions in staff meeting durations and improved communication among internal and external project stakeholders.

The team increases performance from two to nine projects while working less

A construction estimating team attended one of my 'Scrum Lunch and Learn' sessions. After implementing the Scrum framework for a few months, they asked me questions about their adoption. It became a positive coaching relationship, which allowed them to do all the heavy lifting, develop, and reap the professional benefits. The team was then able to reduce weekend work while managing three projects at a time. In other words, they added one project while working less. With some velocity guidance from me, they accelerated and tripled their output. Within 30 days, they took on four more projects. Then, they began training themselves and other teams. When interns arrived that summer, they organized the onboarding training organically without asking for help. Today, this team is capable of working on nine projects at any time and demonstrates a disciplined commitment to continuous improvement. See the graphs below. N equals the number of people on the team.

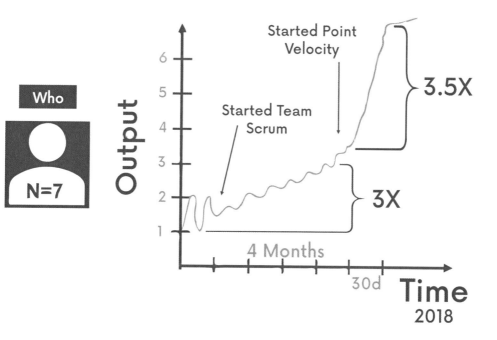

Figure 10.1

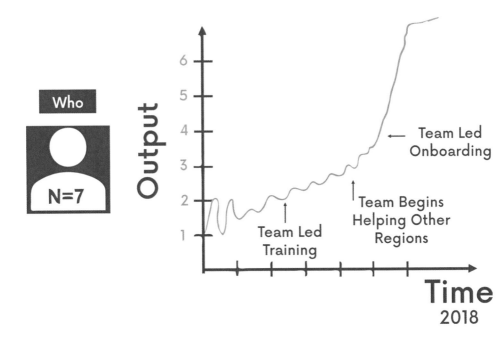

Figure 10.2

Each example above started with people that had never heard of Scrum until meeting me. They learned a little, experimented a lot, and kept improving each Sprint. Be curious and open to new opportunities. Over time your knowledge of Scrum will increase as will your skills and customer satisfaction.

In the next chapter you will learn what makes Scrum unique among other frameworks and why it works so well for design and construction professionals.

Chapter 12
Scrum & Lean: A Power Duo

The required mindset to apply Lean to construction only needs adoption of two principles: **respect for people and continuous improvement.** It's that simple. Both values are embedded inside Scrum. Understanding Lean is foundational. Adopting respect for people and continuous improvement make you a lean practitioner in my humble opinion. "Lean is fundamental to good Scrum." Jeff Sutherland further stated that Scrum's roots are in the 'lean of the grandfathers' which he explained is what we learn from those who came before us that worked to make the world better. Combining lean principles and Scrum powerfully sets you on a path of positive learning and constant adaptation.

I am still practicing lean daily, over a decade and counting, there is no end point. Even after being recognized by the Lean Construction Institute for contributions to them and the greater construction industry in 2019, I still approach work with a child's mind, open and curious. I mentally have the following principles committed to memory for recognition to call them out in my work with teams hard learned on the job delivering complex projects. Simultaneously, my Scrum practice deepened my commitment to practice each of the six Lean Construction Principles daily.

Six Lean Construction Principles

Each of the individual Lean Construction principles combine together to enable more efficient and effective teamwork and project delivery. The foundation of your design and construction Scrum rests on understanding and applying:

1. Respect people

2. Understand your customer's values

3. Create and improve flow

4. Eliminate waste

5. Continuously improve

6. Optimize the system

1. **Respect people**

The most important lean principle is respect: People transform ideas and materials into value. They are at the center of all business interactions. Value yourself first and then extend it to others. This is number one and the sole priority until levels of respect enable healthy people-to-people interactions. I often think of this as my win/win approach with teams new to lean. I demonstrate with actions that I value each person as a trusted partner. Katie Anderson, author of *Learning to Lead, Leading to Learn: Lessons from Toyota Leader Isao Yoshino on a Lifetime of Continuous Learning,* taught me that Respect for People at Toyota means "hold precious what it is to be human." I do not approach people as broken or in need of being fixed. That is a mistake and flawed approach that applies to all supervisors in addition to consultants. Imagine someone coming to you now and telling you that you are "doing it (Scrum, project management, skilled work, marketing, learning, etc.) wrong."

2. **Understand your customer's value**

Does your team know and understand the customer's values? What is important for the customer, and what are his/her expectations? Do not leave this to chance and just assume that you and your team would immensely benefit from a dialogue with your customer about their value. It isn't as simple as budget and schedule. One project owner of one of my past projects told our team repeatedly that money was no object and neither was time. The critical thing for them was building acoustic performance above everything. It was a 1,200 seat performing arts center for a university that would serve generations of future artists. Also, any person or group receiving work in a value stream is a customer, and any handoff between people or groups is customer interaction. Do you know what your supply chain values? If you don't know what your customers value, good. You now have the perfect opportunity to approach them with humble curiosity and engage in meaningful communication. Once you know, share it with your team and broader project partners. Use visuals, such as photos or videos. A picture is worth a thousand words, and, usually, customers will be honored to provide this type of feedback on a photo or a short video. Snapshots from BIM or physical mockups have saturated many conversations about what the customer wants.

3. **Create flow**

Focus on processes and flow. Understanding value allows people to eliminate non-value adding steps, which shortens the process, and improves flow efficiency. Strive for one-piece flow, which is the ideal in any project. Minimize and eliminate multitasking, it is a myth and disrespectful to our human character. Create/ improve your personal flow first before looking around the office or field. Remember, creating value requires the transformation of information or materials. Each of us needs time to make it happen. Block off calendar space daily with individual appointments for deep work. Don't accept meeting requests without agendas and kindly ask others to share why you need to attend. Saying no isn't negative if your presence won't add value. Use reminders for quick tasks – 15 minutes or less to stay organized, meet commitments, and help navigate to delivering more value to your partners and customers. The world is becoming ever more complicated, which requires efficient energy and time management.

4. **Eliminate waste**

Focus on what is of value and stop doing the things that are not. In lean, there are eight types of waste. Remember the acronym DOWNTIME to keep all eight to a minimum and stay in control of your experiences. See chapter 3 for more details.

5. **Continuous improvement.**

Encourage experimentation, learn from manageable failures. FAIL is the first attempt in learning, and learning is how improvement occurs. Not sure how to start? Pick a process and make a standard. Improvement upon standards leads to breakthroughs and innovations. PDCA is the key (keep educating yourself). Practice patience and discipline and remember that you didn't learn to walk without falling down and getting back up. Use the PDCA cycle to enjoy the fruits of your labor.

- Plan a change or test aimed at improvement

- Do carry out the experiment

- Check the results, study and reflect upon your findings

- Act to adopt the change, abandon it, or repeat the cycle

again

6. **Optimize the system**

Optimize the system, not just the parts. A system has inputs, processes, outputs, and often feedback loops. Use Lean tools and methods to help with tactical improvement to benefit the whole project from the customer's perspective. Teams that continuously learn, identify value, and eliminate waste, enjoy massive returns on their efforts that translate directly into their business value. The single greatest way to improve any system is to increase communication and feedback. Optimize your team communication with more frequent interactions that are quick and relevant. Put your project's purpose front and center in meeting rooms or as a regular meeting agenda topic of discussion.

Use Scrum Daily to Improve Your Capacity

Let's think and act together to improve our capacity to deliver value using the Scrum framework. First, we need to know our current capacity by a quick look at where our time is spent during a typical workday. The following list of questions will help illuminate where time is spent.

Non-value-added work tasks	Minutes	Value-added work tasks	Minutes
■ How much time did you spend in meetings where you did not contribute anything?		■ How much time did you spend on communicating timely, accurate, appropriate, and relevant information to the project team?	
■ How much time did you spend answering emails (reading and marking emails for future action is non-value-added time spent)?		■ How much time did you spend leading, guiding, motivating others to manage and overcome issues to achieve project outcomes?	
■ How much time did you spend on the job site versus the project office?		■ How much time did you spend learning?	
■ How much time did you spend updating a status report, spreadsheet, or reviewing timesheets?		■ How much time did you spend managing the deployment and use of people, money, material, equipment, and methods for the project?	
		■ How much time did you spend on problem-solving, making judgments, and decisions to effectively direct the project through changes?	

Non-value-added work tasks	Minutes	Value-added work tasks	Minutes
◘ How much time did you spend tracking the shipment of missing materials onsite?		◘ How much time did you spend on improving the team's culture of respect, responsibility, accountability, honesty, and trust?	
◘ How much time did you spend waiting for information or action from others?			
◘ How much time did you spend making meeting minutes or tracking down open issues log items?		◘ How much time did you spend on planning and scheduling upcoming work?	
◘ How much time did you spend fixing the mistakes of others or your own?		◘ How much time did you spend mentoring and coaching others on the team?	
		◘ How much time do you spend collaborating on upcoming work with the project team?	
Total		Total	

Value-added Time /   x   100 = Value Delivery Capacity %

(Value-added Time + Non-value-added time)

Table 12.1

Now, either start using Scrum individually or with your team. In individual Scrum, you are the Product Owner, Scrum Master, and single Developer. Work inside the framework daily for a week and take another pass through the questions above. If you are starting with your team, work through a single Sprint and then come back and take another pass through the questions above. I did this in 2014 and found that about 80% of my time was in non-value-added tasks. A month after starting Scrum that number was below 30%. You are welcome to come back to this exercise to benchmark and compete with yourself as often as you like.

This next section is for an individual already using Scrum in a team of one or with others. Let's recall what we accomplished and handed off to the next value creator on our project/department/team during our last work day. These questions will become natural and faster to answer as you practice Scrum daily and help others adopt the framework.

Reflection Questions	Felipe's Answers	Your Answers
What increment of value was completed?	25-person meeting preparation with executive sponsor and new meeting facilitator to create a digital engagement space that supports effective communication and engagement	
How long did we work to achieve that increment of value?	Three people working together for a single hour	
How much effort did we put in ? Subjective rating: Low - Medium - High	Medium	
What are we working on today that will help us achieve the next project goal?	Encouraging and supporting the team to make continuous improvement experiments	
Based upon our lean foundation, what change should we make now to enable easier workflow?	Collaborate in a shared document instead of using multiple platforms and resorting to emails and online chat	

Table 12.2

After working through the above thinking and Scrum for a few weeks, now imagine you are at work for ten hours per day. With Scrum, how much more information, materials, or a combination of both did you personally transform for your customer? Is your workday approaching more than 25% value-added activity from the customer's perspective? That is a value view of work. This is one measure of productivity, anything at or above 25% is good. The effectiveness of productive effort, as measured in terms of the rate of value increments (output) per unit individual work (input). Learning curves, interruptions, and unexpected changes decrease our capacity to deliver customer value. Measure your value delivery capacity periodically to see when you cross into more than twice the work in half the time.

With Lean Construction alone, I still worked 60-80 hours per week, not sustainable, and not healthy. Much of that time was wasted in non-value-added work tasks. Being present at work is not a measure nor a proxy for productivity. I took a look at where my time was split between value-added work and non-value-added. Next, I took responsibility to increase my productivity level by first decreasing my time spent in non-value-added activities. Introducing the Scrum framework enabled me to visually see, plan for, and increase value-added work. The questions above will act as a filter for you to reflect on your typical work activities and their level of value. Lean Construction principles and Scrum are a powerful duo. Use them both to operationalize what your project needs to be successful and engage your team to drive towards that success.

In summary, understand the six Lean Construction principles in order. Respect for people begins with self respect. Do one thing at a time. Be realistic with how much you plan to accomplish each day. Don't assume 100% efficiency either, it isn't possible but work towards it anyway. Just becoming aware of opportunities for improvements is typically enough to move your capacity needle in the right direction. Learning which combination of lean principles to apply more into our work, seeing our current capacity, and reflecting on our recent changes is good Scrum in action. We are now shifting towards a habit of inspecting and adapting. Our single workday is a smaller part of our weekly work. Each week is a smaller part of our whole project. In Scrum, our Sprints (typically one to four weeks) combine to cumulatively complete the entire project. These repeating cycles of work are opportunities to improve the work and how we work. We continuously go through this cycle of work, inspection, and adaptation when applying Scrum to enable our daily work.

Chapter 13

Scrum Checklists and Resources

I completely support all Scrum practitioners to begin with sticky notes and markers first. Starting new habits comes with resistance to change so start as simple as possible. There are dozens of online Scrum applications for desktop, laptop, tablet, and mobile phone use. Don't start there if you are not already an experienced user of these applications that market Scrum, Kanban, or Agile workflows. Learn good Scrum first and then adapt the framework to your team's methodology and include software when and if you need to. I work with more Scrum teams that don't use software than those that do. Personally, I use a combination of both. I started using Trello in 2015 after a year of sticky notes in order to keep my Scrum boards with me whether I was at work, at home, or traveling anywhere in between. I receive zero compensation from Trello.

Trello is an online list and card application built by Fog Creek Software in 2011 using Scrum. In 2017, it was purchased by Atlassian, another large software company that uses Scrum. I choose and remain with Trello over dozens of other competitors because they use Scrum to make and update it, plus it's simple, flexible, and designed to promote collaboration. You can also make unlimited cards, have unlimited members on a board or up to ten boards for free. You decide if you want your team's board to be private, invite only, or public to the work.

I organize everything using Scrum and Trello, which helps me and my teams keep engaged with day-to-day project operations, podcast workflows, earning my MBA while working full time, family vacations, and even writing this book. By breaking down work into task-sized parts with checklists, due dates, photos, file attachments, and commenting on cards, Trello has helped me keep good Scrum habits and continuously improve my usage of Scrum.

Trello even has a blog with board examples (Templates) that you can copy and customize in your Trello space. There are workflows with examples in business, design, education, engineering, marketing, project management, and remote work. No matter what your goals are, using Trello will help you and your team to fully use the power of Scrum. I even used visual analytics in Trello to reduce my lead time from nearly 24 days to less than 5 in under a month. The visuals helped me improve my Sprint planning which reduced my lead time by a factor of five. The screenshots below are generated from Trello.

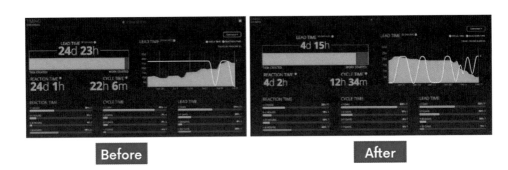

Before   **After**

Figure 13.1

I use this public Scrum Trello Board to help remind and reinforce good Scrum with people I onboard into the framework. It contains examples of design and construction Scrum boards from around the world, videos, online resources, and inspiration.

Felipe's Scrum Trello Resources

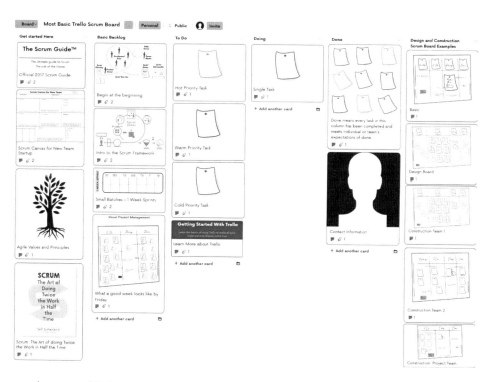

Image 13.1

Chapter 14

Last Planner® System (LPS) and Scrum
One or the other, or both?

When you look into the history of the Last Planner System™ (LPS) of Production Control and Scrum, you'll notice these are both pull systems designed to limit work in progress in order to allow for value-adding work to flow towards the customer. Today, both systems are practiced in design and construction. I personally use them both daily and am responsible for launching new teams into the frameworks. After learning the Scrum framework, I modified how I coach and deploy LPS. Seeing it through the Scrum lens has allowed me to engage teams with a 100% success rate of finishing on schedule or sooner.

System	Last Planner System	Scrum
Definition	The collaborative, commitment-based, planning system that integrates should-can-will-did-learn conversations to make more reliable promises and project delivery. LCI Glossary	Scrum is a lightweight framework that helps people, teams, and organizations generate value through adaptive solutions for complex problems. Scrum Guide
Uses	Design and construction planning and scheduling	Many industries involve complex work such as product development, software, hardware, education, manufacturing, research, science, finance, business, design, construction, and more

Table 14.1

The Last Planners™ are the people that are responsible for the labor, resources, and equipment to prepare assignments for those who do the work. They may also perform work, manage, or do a combination of both. In construction, they are often called "Foremen," "General Foremen," or "Superintendent". In design, you will find the "Architect," "Project Manager," "Design Manager," or "Director." These individuals plan, prepare, and supervise work.

In Scrum, team members are autonomous and are part of the planning, preparations, and supervision. The Scrum Master may be any of the design and construction roles. This individual is the servant leader and keeper of the Scrum processes and philosophy. Last Planners may be thought of as Scrum Masters for their teams. They both ensure work is safe, solve problems, and find ways to make the workflow.

In my experience, projects managed by either LPS, Scrum, or a combination of both outperform traditional project management jobs. These teams report they spend far less time fire fighting and far more time pulling in work at higher quality with less effort.

LPS is most typically taught by facilitators that learned from the early developers of the system, the Lean Construction Institute's approved Instructors, or the Associated General Contractors of America via the Certificate of Management-Lean Construction (CM-Lean). I am a product of the first two. Scrum is very often self taught and training organizations exist worldwide for guided learning in addition to a vast number of free resources online. I highly recommend you know the source's credentials. I learn from direct sources whenever possible. Dr. Jeff Sutherland taught me how to be a Scrum Master. Glenn Ballard, Kristin Hill, and Dan Fauchier taught me how to be an LPS coach and facilitator.

I asked Jeff Sutherland what advice he would give to people who learn about Scrum and are not sure if they should use it. He recommended just trying it to experience the positive impact it would have on their work.

Then I asked JJ Sutherland, CEO of Scrum Inc. where people should start with Scrum. He suggested the following steps:

1. Prioritize.

2. Don't try to do everything at once. Figure out what's the most important thing, get that done first and then go on to the next.

It is a fact that waiting times cause a lot of waste in construction. JJ also suggested we prioritize first, then focus, and use Scrum's framework to keep us from getting distracted.

In LPS, many experienced coaches like Joe Donarumo and Frank Coln start with the Daily Standup Meeting. This is very similar to the Daily Scrum. This 15-minute meeting helps teams communicate and create a system to raise constraints that are impacting the workflow. From there the team will gain the capacity to implement more parts of LPS.

In a nutshell, whether you use LPS or Scrum, the most important step is to get started and then reiterate over time until you utilize the entire framework to optimize your project outcomes. Don't wait for permission to take the first step.

In either system, it is required to ask for permission to take the first step. Earlier in my career, as a project manager on a $70 million-dollar hard bid, 88,000 square-foot performing arts university theater construction project, I read Jeff's red book, *Scrum: The Art of Doing Twice the Work in Half the Time*. First I took in the audio book narrated by JJ Sutherland and then bought the hardcover book to dive deeper. Within a week of finishing the book, I was practicing Scrum, alone. My project team didn't want any part of it and I still used the framework to organize and accomplish all my general contractor management duties. I went from working late evenings and weekends to only working about 50 hours per week and spending nearly half of the day on the project site helping the superintendent resolve bottlenecks and constraints. Simultaneously I took on leadership roles in training and with resolving a past project undergoing litigation. That is much more than twice the work in half the time. I also used LPS, a Lean Construction framework, for some phases of the project. For LPS we needed buy-in from the trades and from the general contractor's leaders. Both systems create pull for work and limit work in progress that hinders flow. With my experience, I now see individual trades practicing LPS on projects even when the general contractor doesn't.

The book *Scrum: The Art of Doing Twice the Work in Half the Time* by Jeff and JJ Sutherland demonstrates that we can use Scrum to change how we work and how teams deliver value across many different industries. The appendix lists out two handfuls of steps to get you and a Scrum team started. You can read the book or my adapted version for construction online.

Construction Scrum Case Studies

The 2020 Scrum Guide lists four consolidated steps starting with a Scrum Master to foster the right conditions for:

1. A Product Owner to prioritize the work for a project into a Product Backlog.

2. The Scrum Team to take the top portion of work into an Increment of value during a Sprint.

3. The Scrum Team and its stakeholders to inspect the outputs of their work cycle and adjust their work and processes for the next Sprint.

4. The Scrum Team to repeat the process.

LPS publications typically end with a summary of how to better align the work with the project schedule and increase reliable promises to complete work. The following five conversations in LPS correlate to five levels of planning including:

1. Defining Project Milestone and Phase Schedules (Should)

2. Single Phase Scheduling to Process Workflows, Look-ahead Schedules (Can)

3. Processing Workflows to Operations, Weekly Work Plans (Will)

4. Operations to Tasks, Daily Coordination (Did)

5. Tasks to Elemental Motion, Learning and Actions (Learn)

If you are newer to either framework, invest the time to study the visual representations below.

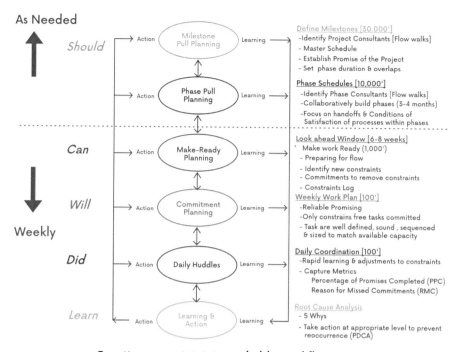

Creating an maintaining reliable workflow

Figure 14.1, *LPS Schematic*

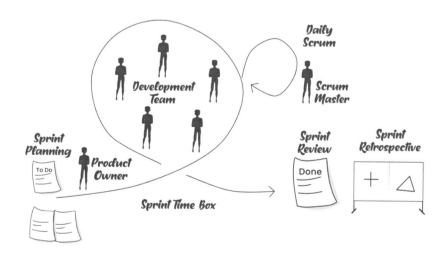

Figure 14.2, *Scrum Framework*

Both frameworks have many similarities but, at first glance, the vocabulary seems unique. I use both systems. In my daily work I use Scrum to serve my organization and also manage my podcast. With teams, some ask for LPS or Scrum. A few ask for both. Those that ask for both use them together. Each framework relies on a cycle of time for work. Design and construction most often follow a monthly cycle. Scrum usually follows a weekly or biweekly cycle. The original Scrum guide recommended a six-week work cycle, aka Sprint.

In the 2020 Scrum Guide, you will find the following:

"Sprints enable predictability by ensuring inspection and adaptation of progress toward a Product Goal at least every calendar month. When a Sprint's horizon is too long the Sprint Goal may become invalid, complexity may rise, and risk may increase. Shorter Sprints can be employed to generate more learning cycles and limit risk of cost and effort to a smaller time frame. Each Sprint may be considered a short project."

The Sprint duration is just a cycle of time. Again, it could be a single work week, it could be every two weeks, it could be every month. There are good reasons for why you stay steady a given cycle of time. At the end of the cycle, you and your team need to be able to deliver an increment of value to the owner or next member in the value stream. LPS was invented by Glen Ballard and Greg Howell in the 1980s to help large commercial construction projects improve schedule reliability. The system was formalized and made public in the 1990s.

Coincidentally, Scrum was invented by Dr. Jeff Sutherland in the

1980s and later improved with the help of Ken Schwaber before being made public in 1995. Both frameworks focus on human conversations and interactions. Each framework provides scaffolding for consistently positive human interaction and the constant flow of work among value creators. The results are more reliable, and much more predictable planning, scheduling, and execution can happen compared to traditional waterfall scheduling.

The figure below includes both frameworks with the LPS parts set adjacent to the Scrum parts.

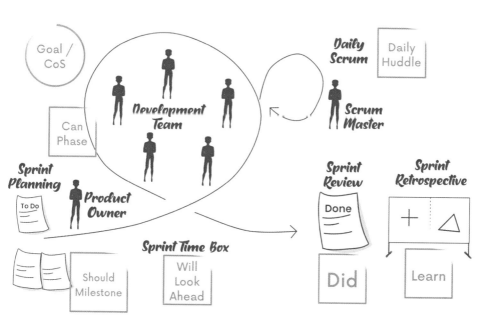

Figure 14.3, **LPS Superimposed on Scrum**

I see and understand LPS through the Scrum framework. The five LPS conversations flow along the Scrum framework perfectly. The first LPS conversation begins with what we **should** do. Start on the bottom left of the diagram, identify what the work is, aka the backlog. Both in design and construction terminology and in Scrum the term Backlog is used. It combines all the tasks that we **should** do in order to complete this build or project, which could be a hospital, a school, a bridge, a road, sidewalks, a playground, a solar array, a wastewater treatment plant, an airport terminal, a tenant improvement, or any type of construction, or renovation.

Sprint planning is the next step, answering what we **can** do in a work cycle, aka Sprint. The team accomplishes this planning effort in a meeting by pulling tasks off the backlog and turn them into milestones. A starting and ending milestone generate the beginning and ending of a given phase. The project serves a goal for the owner, and the team uses value statements or conditions of satisfaction to help determine project goals. In Scrum we make Sprint goals to guide what is in and out of a given Sprint. The Sprint time box gives the team a look-ahead schedule and answers what we **will** do. It's very common in construction to use a three-week to six-week schedule as a guide for the upcoming work. In design, one-week and two-week schedules are more common in earlier design phases and become more synchronized with construction durations in the more detailed design stage.

The Daily Scrum is the same as the Daily Huddle in LPS. In Scrum the meeting is facilitated by the Scrum Master or Team Captain. This meeting answers what we **did** each day. In LPS the team notes what tasks were completed as planned and reasons for variance for those that were not completed. This process generates the weekly Plan Percent Complete,

PPC, and variance metrics. Variances may include prerequisite work not complete, design issue/RFI, failed inspection, labor not available, material not available, equipment not available, change order work, submittals, weather, unforeseen conditions, etc. The Sprint Review closes the cycle down and stakeholders experience the completed increment of value. This is the close of the work week in LPS and the cumulative metrics are recorded for the week indicating what the team **did**. Just like in Scrum, the Sprint Review meeting is open to anybody and everybody, it has the spirit of a kindergarten show and tell. Scrum ends with the Retrospective meeting for team **learning**. And so does the Sprint Review meeting. The purpose is to reveal what went well, what can be better, what process can we improve, and how fast is our team delivering value.

The makers of LPS invented it to help improve the reliability of project schedules to help people design and install the right work at the right time. Scrum was invented to deliver the highest possible value in the shortest amount of time. Similar but not exactly identical. I find Scrum more effective and have come to view LPS through the lens of the Scrum framework. I've known and practiced LPS twice as long but learning Scrum immediately improved my LPS strategy and tactics. Teams I coach improve upon their critical path schedules without exception. I know many LPS coaches and facilitators that use a variety of methods with an equal variety of results, some good, some not.

The Common Critical Path method

Let's look at an example starting with the construction industry's common practice, the **Critical Path** (CPM) method, a waterfall schedule. The name came up due to the Gantt chart. These types of bar charts with gravity look similar to a waterfall cascading from the top left corner to the bottom right. The work tasks are logically tied and organized by successor and predecessor tasks. The logic connections are available in most CPM scheduling software applications. I've used this approach with design teams, construction teams, and mixed teams with and without all stakeholder participation. Let's take this corporate office building schedule as our example. This project is fictitious but the durations and activities are based on historical data from major United States city construction projects.

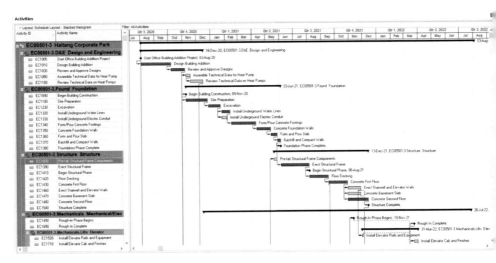

Image 14.1, *CPM Schedule*

In this typical waterfall schedule, we've got to finish one activity to start the next. Arrows connect subsequent activities in a logical order and red-colored bars mark the critical path. You can read all the activities in sequence to see that the office building addition starts after the design of that addition is complete. Next, the project enters into a review and approval phase starting early October through to early November. For those of you seeing a CPM schedule like this one for the first time, the critical path (the red bars) is determined by an algorithm that calculates which tasks have no buffers and must complete as scheduled or the whole project will be delayed. Conversely, the project finishes faster if any red-bar activities finish sooner assuming no other tasks take longer. In technical terms, these red-bar tasks have zero float. For example, if the forming and pouring concrete takes one day longer than scheduled, it creates a cascade effect through the entire schedule causing the forecasted end day to be one day longer. The black bars are rollup summaries called **Hammocks**. The grey descriptions above the white tasks are called **Work Breakdown Structure (WBS)** headings that group certain tasks to make the schedule easier to read.

It is better practice to have conditions of satisfaction for an LPS session. Conditions of Satisfaction in Lean Construction are explicit descriptions of all the actual requirements that must be satisfied by the team members in order to deliver value to the customer. Examples could be "safe project delivery, zero injuries" or "everyone makes a fair profit." In Scrum we start each Sprint with a goal. I find that specific session goals are more impactful. For this schedule let's set the goal to be:

"The last Haitang employee moved in by August 3, 2022."

Sharing the session goal with all participants enables greater creativity and alignment on the milestones that aid in achieving the big goal. The team discusses this goal during the session and agrees that it means that the last employee is going to move into this fully functional building, all systems work, and all required approvals are met.

Then, we identify the project milestones and focus on the ones that come up next. We transfer them to sticky notes and place them on a timeline like the one below ideally on a whiteboard or a similar highly visual medium.

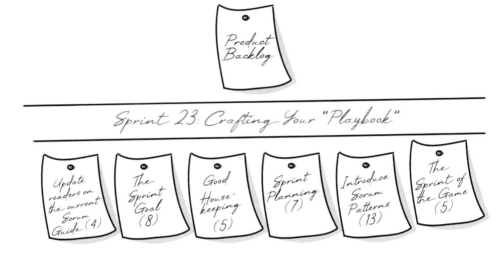

Figure 14.4, **Project Milestones**

I also recommend creating monthly milestones for longer projects and at shorter intervals for projects less than a year. Use your construction experience or ask the participants to establish some milestones based on the start or end of the WBS sections. Employ your imagination to define the milestones, which signify the end of a phase or beginning of a new phase. Use adjectives and dates to make them more descriptive. I've witnessed many projects improve their schedules just by applying this part of LPS with Scrum principles. Making the work more visual, collaborating on the sequence, and discussing goals makes the planning process more meaningful and easier to understand. You can also look at the milestones in a Scrum board view. I personally use the timeline view with teams and mentally keep this board view with the goal in mind.

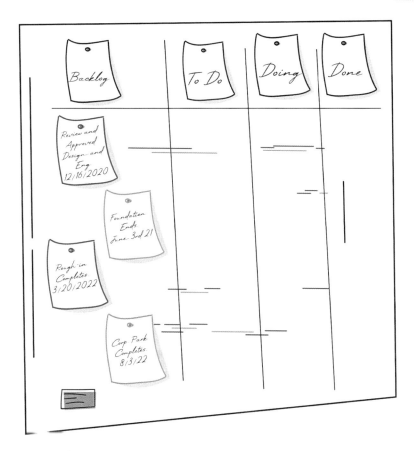

Figure 14.5, Milestone Scrum Board

Some teams prefer bar charts, others a visual timeline or Scrum board. It's your choice. Use what you and your team feel most comfortable with. Then, together with your team, determine the best sequence for the phase before you add tasks, commitments, and dates.

LPS, like in Scrum, moves from long-term thinking to shorter term actions. It organizes a phase of work between a start and end milestone. The team further breaks down the work into tasks that become the To Do list items. The sequence between the tasks, the phase, is based on a priority order set by the team. Next, the phase planning or pull planning begins with the end state, the target milestone, in mind.

In a timeline view, the team begins with the first milestone on the far left, which is the releasing or enabling condition. Whether you use Last Planner or Scrum, you create the activities that follow in the figure below. Tasks that are stacked happen at nearly the same time but the topmost tag has priority.

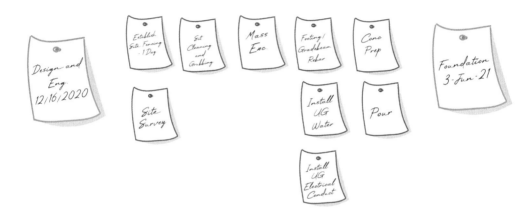

Figure 14.6, **Phase Pull Plan**

Going back to our example, the site clearing and grubbing begins after the site survey is complete and so on for the rest of the tasks until finally foundations are complete on June 3, 2021. Then, the mass excavation follows. The tags are color-coded to match a key for each company. I think of a phase pull plan like this as a Scrum board. The activities in this way indicate a sequence, handoff points, and the company/responsible person.

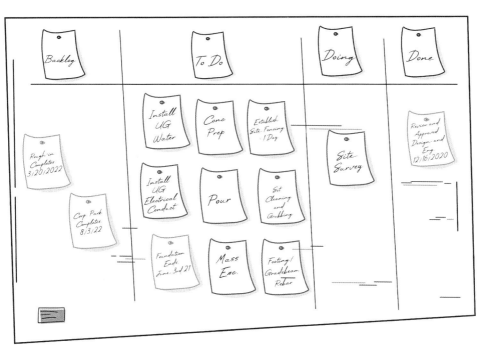

Figure 14 7, *Phase Scrum Board*

We are incrementally building upon the milestone conversation. Next, we have the phase populated in the Sprint Backlog commonly called the To Do list. When the team completes the To Do list, they complete a phase between two milestones, to make the sample schedule's Design and Engineering WBS an action, combine that with the schedule activity to make a tag that reads, "Design and Engineering Approval and Foundations." Each completed phase is a step closer towards the end goal. You can certainly get more detailed by adding in dates and changing the timeline to look like a calendar. However, I recommend starting in a basic timeline and iterating with the team into greater organized views. During a planning session, the LPS facilitator or Scrum Master will focus on the handoffs between any two companies. This allows people to focus on the main pieces of work rather than argue about how long things will take. The idea behind this collaboration is to optimize the best possible sequence to achieve the goal of the next milestone. In our example the goal is that all employees have moved into the corporate office building by August 3, 2022. Everything ties back towards that end goal or ultimate condition of satisfaction. That's how I learned to more deeply understand LPS and how I use Scrum to enable better flow with teams.

A valuable aspect of Scrum is purposely working in shorter increments such as a week or two versus eight-week schedules which many construction teams use. Shorter intervals allow for faster learning. Mistakes in the process made in one week are raised and marked for improvement for the next cycle of work. Working in long iterations greater than a month doesn't support reflection and rapid learning. If we are on a 12-month schedule and only make updates once a month, we only get a maximum of 12 chances to improve the process. If we are on a biweekly planning and scheduling cycle, we get 24 chances to improve. Shorter iterations are an advantage that Scrum has over LPS. Applying the Scrum framework to LPS allows you and your team to get feedback, make improvements, and continue iterating each Sprint or work cycle towards the goal.

Commercial construction projects typically last more than a year and typical work cycles last a monthI recommend a pull planning session with the team at least once a month. Every four weeks, which are a natural cycle in design and construction, you can set the Sprint to coincide with the project's monthly billing. In an early design project phase, when the design is not yet detailed, cycle times should be shorter, such as weekly or bi-weekly. The less detailed the design, the more often planning is required. People using Scrum pull activities forward and complete the work. Conversations shift from telling people when they have to finish their tasks towards collaborating to when they can start and how they can support each other.

Sharing information is vital for project success

Both frameworks also improve information sharing and communication. The Daily Huddle and Daily Scrum are 15-minute meetings. All involved parties are participating. The agenda usually covers the past, present, and future work.

Questions may be:

- 🏠 What work did we accomplish yesterday?

- 🏠 What's our team working on today?

- 🏠 What impediments or constraints are blocking us from proceeding?

Each of the questions is in relation to the team's goal. The daily meeting is also a great starting point to begin using either LPS or Scrum with a team. It is typically held in the morning hours to start the day as a team focused on the goal. The best teams use their Scrum or LPS boards to check in either LPS tags, Scrum tags, or constraints. Using visual boards allows people to look towards the impediments, roadblocks, or constraints rather than seeing a person as the problem. This brief meeting enables effective communication, requests for help, and rapid sharing of what is happening across the project. I've witnessed teams of 50 snap through this meeting in less than 15 minutes when they follow a script and use a board with their tags. There are good and better practices for issue escalations such as parking lots. Some people like to use issue tracking logs as well. Just be sure to use a consistent practice so people can come together and solve problems in a separate meeting when needed.

Teams working in either framework get to know each other and depend upon each other at a much higher level than the transactional nature of traditional project delivery. In my experience, anytime I was working on a team with frustrated, misunderstood, and unhappy people, mistakes and accidents were more common along with higher levels of turnover and burnout. Team morale absolutely impacts quality and productivity. If you have high emotional intelligence, you can gauge team morale very easily. If you want to be more scientific, you can use anonymous surveys periodically to assess it, share it with the team, and work to make improvements. There are various ways to measure the team's sense of engagement, and Lean Construction and Scrum teams alike use a simple subjective five-point scale (1-Very Unhappy to 5-Very Happy) for "happiness." Happiness wraps in the overall working environment, expectations, and progress on improvement efforts. Ending the survey with an open ended survey question such as, "What else should the team know or consider?" That the team works to improve sends a message that the team is autonomous and that individual well-being is respected.

Metrics to track performance

Both frameworks also include some metrics. LPS uses Percent Plan Complete (PPC). It is a reverse looking metric of how well promises were kept. If our LPS team had a weekly plan for 10 tasks and we accomplished eight, our PPC would be $(8/10) \times 100 = 80\%$. The 80% PPC tells the team what occurred during the last work cycle. It is a team measure and should not be used to individually rank companies. Projects are complex and interconnected. PPC is a team metric. Typical CPM scheduling has a 48 to 54% chance of being completed as scheduled. That is about equivalent to a coin flip. The PPC metric plotted over time gives teams a better sense of how reliable they are performing. PPC is not a letter grade, which I recommend sharing explicitly with your teams. Teams that achieve PPC even as low as 60% still gain and improve completion of milestones as compared to the CPM schedule dates.

The other metric is variance, any deviation from plan. Integrated project delivery (IPD) teams typically track PPC, variance, and team health. Projects also track other key performance indicators on budget, schedule, or quality. Scrum uses a similar metric, called velocity, to measure team speed. Velocity is a measure of the amount of work a Scrum Team can accomplish during a single Sprint. Like PPC in LPS, it is calculated at the end of the Sprint (LPS weekly work cycle) by totaling the points for all fully completed Sprint Backlog Items.

Let's say that we planned to do ten equally-sized, one-point tasks, and we only moved eight of them to the Done column by the end of the Sprint, the team's velocity would be eight. Velocity like PPC plotted over time can help a Scrum Master and Product Owner predict if their team is slowing down, maintaining the course, or speeding up. Not all Scrum teams use velocity and not all LPS teams use PPC. Most of the high-performing teams do. You don't have to use metrics on day one with a new team but you should absolutely be iterating your way there over time.

I have studied and used both systems for years. I find that looking at the financial success of the project also only tells the story of the project's past. It cannot predict what is going to happen, especially early on during the beginning of a project. Evaluating happiness as a metric better predicts the future. Leaders that care to listen and keep a pulse of what's happening with the people doing the work more quickly notice trends and can help the team adapt or pivot. If you notice a dip in team happiness, you can quickly change course. If you notice a dip in financial metrics, you will need to do more analysis and possibly interview many team members to stop further financial decline in performance. Team health seems to be more accurate than team happiness.

The Last Planner System of Production Control and Scrum are both frameworks designed to pull increments of value added work into progress while simultaneously limiting work in progress. I actively practice using both, and many organizations are adopting them as well to enable complex project delivery with increased reliability in design and construction. If you have experience with either system, I invite you to see them through my experiences with Scrum. If you have any questions about Scrum or the Last Planner System that aren't answered in this book or on my YouTube channel, please contact me. Thank you for reading this book. I would like to leave you with one question: How will you integrate LPS into your Scrum framework?

Key Takeaways Part III

1. Awareness is the first step to initiate change and the key to Scrum success. Become aware of your experiences and start reflecting on what is holding you back from using Scrum successfully. Check awareness levels by quickly rating each of the three areas you learned that prevent most people and teams from beginning. Start where the awareness is highest first before moving outside of your span of control/influence. Remember, you have my permission to start using Scrum, your team and organization will follow your adoption.

	Low		Medium		High
Individual Awareness	1	2	3	4	5
Team Awareness	1	2	3	4	5
Organization Awareness	1	2	3	4	5

Table 14.2

Start using Scrum today. Take the framework one piece at a time. You can run a short staff meeting using the Scrum framework. Iterate your way to design and construction value delivery.

2. Make small changes daily to adjust how fast you want to shift towards more value and less waste. Setting long and intermediate milestones will help you celebrate the wins and see how far you have left to go. Shifting from firefighting today's problems to planning tomorrow's wins is a different mindset. Be patient, make daily progress. Putting these Lean Construction techniques in three steps set me on a path of continuous improvement.

Learn and understand each of the **Six Lean Construction Principles**

1. Respect people

2. Understand your customer's values

3. Create and improve flow

4. Eliminate waste

5. Continuously improve

6. Optimize the system

- How much time do you spend on value-added work?

- How much time do you spend on non-value-added work?

- Is my Value Delivery Capacity approaching 25%

Value Delivery Capacity % =

[Value-added Time / (Value-added Time + Non-value-added time)] x 100

3. Use a combination Scrum and the Last Planner System of Production Controls (LPS) to pull increments of value-added work to completion while enabling smoother workflows. Complex project delivery doesn't need complex systems. Use both frameworks to increase reliability in design and construction project success.

System	Last Planner System of Production Controls (LPS)	Scrum
Definition	The collaborative, commitment-based, planning system that integrates should-can-will-did-learn conversations to make more reliable promises and project delivery.	Scrum is a lightweight framework that helps people, teams, and organizations generate value through adaptive solutions for complex problems.
Uses	Design and construction planning and scheduling	Design and construction planning and scheduling plus many other industries

Table 14.3

Scrum enables even better LPS. Seek to understand the pulse of what's happening with the people doing the work on your project. Is morale high or low? Are you using either or both systems correctly? Do you need to engage an experienced coach? Learn each framework by using it directly. Start with a small part of your project. This will allow for the team to more notice trends, adapt, pivot, and get help early when needed.

Conclusion

Construction Scrum, Deliver Projects Easier, Better, and Faster

When you begin using Scrum, you will most probably hear the word "no" a lot. Don't let it hinder your productivity increasing efforts. Buildings don't build themselves, people do. Scrum gives people a consistent way to self-organize, lead, and deliver value on complex work. Whether you are a beginner with the framework or an experienced Scrum user, face each "no" with respect, openness, courage, focus, and commitment. Adopting all five Scrum values will help you collaborate better with others and deliver more value overall. Just begin, start small, improve every sprint, and adapt the framework to create better results with your construction team.

I sincerely appreciate my mentors, industry partners, and genuine friends that respectfully challenged me to learn, adapt, and improve daily. Becoming a committed lean practitioner in 2008 is the greatest title I am still working to retain each day. Over ten years of experience implementing lean on a variety of construction projects, business processes, construction industry partner firms, academia, research, and non-construction organizations most positively improved me holistically. One I started in construction, I only ever worked on a single project. Some were better than others. After adopting lean, all were great projects. After adopting Scrum I was able to give back and help improve the construction industry. Today I get weekly messages of gratitude and appreciation from owners, designers, contractors, researchers, supply chain partners, teachers, and students for my contributions to transforming their work and the industry at large.

In the first five years I had doubled my output. In other words, I maintained my deliverables and work productivity output while using 40 hours less per week to do it. I was enjoying my work more, being more helpful to my team and company, yet being present for my family and personal commitments as a husband, father, brother, son, and friend. My effectiveness fluctuates somewhat today with business travel and varied demand for engagements, yet I've continued to experience exponential output improvements year-round. One example of this occurred from 2017-2018. In 18 months, I earned my AACSB-accredited MBA while continuing to work full time and taking on an additional 20 hours of schoolwork per week. I did this without missing any work deadlines, maintaining top grades in each course, and balancing my health and family time.

My philosophy and relationship with my work changed. That changed the people I learned from, followed, and who followed me. Those interactions led to more changes and improvements in my work processes and, ultimately, to breakthroughs in my capacity, which allowed me to continue accelerating my professional development and skills. The choice is yours and yours alone. Join thousands of other construction professionals that repeatedly improve their work and simultaneously increase their creative freedom to grow and succeed. You already got my permission at the start of this book to learn, experiment, and repeat for greater customer value delivery individually, in teams, organizations, and our industry at-large. Will you reap the benefits of your efforts using Scrum, or will you stay dreaming about the possibilities? Either choice will yield both measurable and noticeable results. Start small, get better every sprint, and build your capabilities with others in the growing construction Scrum community.

 # BIBLIOGRAPHY

Liker, J and Meier, D. (2006, pg. 64). *The Toyota Way Fieldbook: A practical guide for implementing Toyota's 4P's*. New York: McGraw-Hill Education.

Richards, Chet. (2004). *Certain to Win*. Xlibris.

Sutherland, Dr. Jeff. (2014). *Scrum: The art of doing twice the work in half the time*. Crown Business.

Sutherland, Dr. Jeff and Coplien, James O. (2019). *A Scrum Book: The Spirit of the Game*. 1st Edition.

Weinberg, Gerald. (1991). *Quality Software Management: Volume 1 Systems Thinking*. Dorset House

Womack, J and Jones, Daniel T. 2nd edition (June 1, 2003) *Lean Thinking: Banish Waste and Create Wealth in Your Corporation*. Free Press.

ABOUT THE AUTHOR

A serial entrepreneur, Felipe Engineer-Manriquez is an International keynote speaker and practitioner with over two decades of experience in process improvement, project planning and execution, change management, and employee engagement in the construction industry. Over the past ten years, he also helped organizations implement business strategies.

He is currently serving as the national Lean Construction Program leader for a multi-billion-dollar general contractor engaging at project and enterprise level for improvements. As a business professional, Engineer-Manriquez uses proven operations management to guide regional and multi-regional teams to generate multi-billion-dollar new business leads from new and existing clients in healthcare and manufacturing.

He works with executives on strategic planning and improving work processes to ensure safety, quality, production, and net margin increase. He also coaches construction professionals, designers/engineers, and project teams across the nation.

Engineer-Manriquez is a Dr. Jeff Sutherland trained Scrum Master with years of weekly sprints moved to "Done." He is also a Registered Scrum Trainer™ (RST). RSTs are the only Scrum Trainers endorsed by Dr. Jeff Sutherland. The Agile Education Program powered by Scrum Inc. ™, provides Agile from the Source. It is the only training curriculum endorsed by the co-creator of Scrum & creator of Scrum@Scale. The Design and Construction Registered Scrum Master™ (RSM) curriculum was co-created by Felipe Engineer-Manriquez with the Agile Education Program team. It enables RSM graduates to deliver design and construction project value and be recognized in the International Registry of Agile Professionals™. Felipe shares his Scrum knowledge worldwide with construction professionals through The EBFC Show podcast, Blogs, interactive education programs, and conferences.

Felipe has a Bachelor of Science in Electrical Engineering and a Master of Business Administration. He holds active leadership roles in the Lean Construction Institute, Construction Industry Institute, and other business organizations.

Felipe is an approved instructor/facilitator of the Lean Construction Institute (LCI). He was honored with the LCI Chairman's Award during the 21st Annual LCI Congress (2019) for contributions to the Institute and the design and construction industry as a whole. He was a founding member of the St. Louis Lean Construction Institute Community of

Practice where he is serving as Vice-Chair (2018-2021) and has been an annual Congress Team Scrum Master since 2018. Felipe also co-founded the Kaiser Permanente Southern California and Northern California Lean Construction Communities of Practice.

Felipe Engineer-Manriquez served as the chair of the Construction Industry Institute (CII) Collaborative Scheduling Research Team (18-362) from 2018-2020. The team used the Scrum framework based on the work by Dr. Jeff Sutherland and Ken Schwaber as published in The Scrum Guide™. Felipe, RT-362 Chair, acted as the team's Scrum Master and onboarded each team member into the framework. In 2019, the team met in-person every other month for 1.5-days until 2020 when COVID-19 required the team to further adapt and change to online meetings. The team alternated conference calls every other month and tracked all work in a digital Scrum board. CII appointed Felipe Engineer-Manriquez to their Funded Studies Committee and Board of Advisors in early 2021 in recognition of outstanding leadership RT-362 and inspired use of Scrum for managing CII's portfolio of research projects.

His passion is to inspire, engage, and activate the next generation of California's construction workforce by speaking to students and job seekers for Build California, Associated General Contractors of CA's comprehensive workforce development program. Ambassadors participate in both virtual and in-person classroom presentations, jobsite visits, and career fairs at high schools across the state.

Felipe was born and grew up outside of Chicago where he also met his wife, Allamai. They have been happily adventuring together for nearly three decades and live in California with their son, Noah. Today, you can find them just outside of Sacramento walking nature trails or playing in the garden.

LICENSES & CERTIFICATIONS

- Registered Scrum Trainer™ (RST)

- Registered Scrum Master™ (RSM)

- Scrum Alliance Certified ScrumMaster (CSM)

- Registered Product Owner™ (RPO)

- Registered Scrum@Scale Practitioner™ (RS@SP)

- The Tuck School of Business at Dartmouth - Field Of Study Developing Breakthrough Innovations with the Three Box Solution

- edX HarvardX Contract Law

- KAIZEN Academy KAIZEN Green Belt

- U.S. Dept. of Labor Occupational Safety and Health Administration OSHA 30-Hour

- Project Management Institute (PMI) Project Management Professional (PMP)®

Continue Sprinting with Me

Do you want to hear from industry professionals how they have embraced Scrum in their work and teams? Subscribe to The EBFC Show Podcast today! The website includes interviews, blogs, how-to videos, and training classes.

www.theebfcshow.com

The Easier, Better, for Construction Show strives to make building easier and better today. We dig into design and construction topics to inspire you to develop your people, improve your processes, and take the business of building to the next level.

Made in the USA
Monee, IL
27 November 2024